LANDING YOUR DREAM GRAD SCHOOL

A Step-by-step Guide to the US Master's and Doctoral School Application Process for Domestic and International Applicants.

Tulli Ariyaratne, Ph.D.

Landing Your Dream Grad School
A Step-by-step Guide to the US Master's and Doctoral School Application Process for Domestic and International Applicants.

Copyright © Tulli Ariyaratne (2024)

ISBN: 979-8-9902605-4-2 (Paperback)

For permission requests, write to,
tulli@learnwithtulli.com

Cover design: Olina @olinart

Learnwithtulli.com

Dedication

To my loving Mom and Dad for being my pillars of strength, love, and support, and for their inspiration.

To my husband Trent for believing in me and being the light of my life.

FORWARD

Entering graduate school is a significant milestone in one's academic and professional life. Being accepted to the best graduate program marks the beginning of a new adventure of personal growth, research, and knowledge. Finding the correct graduate program can be hard. There are so many graduate schools, and you need to identify which best program suits your requirements and will prepare you for your future endeavors. In this book, you'll find in detail a step-by-step guide for choosing, applying to, and getting accepted to the perfect grad school. Whether you are considering a master's or doctoral program, in pursuit of a career change, or aiming to deepen your expertise in a particular field, this book is written to illuminate the path towards successful admission to the graduate school of your dreams.

With unique requirements, deadlines, and expectations, the landscape of graduate school admission can be challenging. However, armed with the right knowledge, strategies, and resources, you can confidently navigate this terrain and position yourself as a strong candidate among a competitive pool of applicants. This book provides tips and tactics that most graduate applicants miss and provides instructions to bring you to the top among other applicants.

Throughout this book, you will discover practical advice, expert tips, and proven strategies to optimize every aspect of your application, from drafting a compelling statement of purpose, to choosing the right person to recommend you, preparing for standardized tests, and acing admissions interviews. You will find insights on choosing the right program, navigating financial aid options, and managing the transition to graduate school life. This practical advice is given by a person (me) who attended three graduate schools in the United States with zero tuition fees and zero student debt. I have been a graduate student, earned my master's and PhD, and am now working in a university as an educator and a researcher. So you can trust me. While this book offers a roadmap to grad school admission, it could also be your companion on your journey towards academic and professional fulfillment. This book may be a great inspiration and guide if you are lost and exhausted after your undergraduate studies and do not know what to do next.

Above all, pursuing knowledge is a great endeavor. As you embark on this intellectual journey, may this book be a source of inspiration and a great companion on your grad school admission process. This book will make a meaningful great impact on your academic and professional life. While many apply to graduate school, there are not many books or resources on graduate school admission. Due to the lack of guidance, many applicants fail to get accepted to their dream grad schools, even though they are fully qualified. This book will fill that gap.

This book is a good fit for anyone who has an undergraduate degree or is completing an undergraduate degree. If you are a parent or a relative of a career-focused teen, this book may help them someday find their ideal grad school and get accepted to it. This book would be a great gift for anyone graduating with their college degree. If you do not have any academic qualification, but are still curious, you are warmly welcomed to read it as well. I am confident that anyone who reads this book will be able to understand all the tips and the trends that top ranking grad programs follow to admit grad students their programs. If you find any information in this book that needs to be reviewed or edited, please write to us at *tulli@learnwithtulli.com*. We highly value your comments. Best wishes on your journey to graduate school and beyond. The adventure awaits. Embrace it and let your future shine.

Tulli Ariyaratne,
Dublin, Ohio, USA.

TABLE OF CONTENTS

LIST OF TABLES

CHAPTER 1

THE START

When beginning to consider a grad-level qualification, you may feel intimidated or unsure. Unfortunately, people in your life may even discourage you from pursuing higher education. Friends and colleagues, especially those without a master's degree or PhD, may speak negatively about your ambitions. However, graduate-level education offers incredible advantages. With a grad-level qualification, you may earn greater income, experience a higher reputation, and have access to better opportunities than you would without one. Your grad school journey could be one of the most memorable and enjoyable times of your life, as it was for me. During grad school, I forged friendships that I still maintain today. I met well-known faculty and world-renowned scholars and thrived in the learning environment of a large research university. For knowledge seekers, graduate school offers unparalleled intellectual, relational, and vocational opportunities.

In this commercialized world, corporations and academic institutions look for paper qualifications. Some may not agree with me, but a simple online search of job openings will demonstrate that businesses always ask for minimum qualifications — mostly academic — which serve as a gatekeepers. While it is relatively simple to gain new skills, earning a degree takes time, holding people back from better positions and more fulfilling careers. I have met longstanding employees who miss promotions because they lack post-baccalaureate qualifications. I have met people in academia who stagnate in the same position because they do not have a terminal degree.

While some believe that an undergraduate degree is sufficient for success, the truth is that it is not always enough. If you want to reach the top of the career ladder, you need graduate-level qualifications. You will likely even need graduate-level qualifications for promotions. I am not saying that you must have a graduate degree to sustain yourself; there are many good people who do not have a graduate degree but still achieve their goals. However, it is clear that graduate degrees offer many advantages. Stop reading, and reflect on the benefits and opportunities that have opened to you because of your undergraduate degree. Compare your life with the lives of your high school colleagues who only earned their high school diploma. Notice the opportunities and benefits available to you because of your undergraduate qualification. The same is true for master's and doctoral studies, it is a gateway to abundant opportunities.

Career Development

In many fields, graduate qualifications are required for professionals to advance in their careers. You will be able to find a job that suits you with just an undergraduate degree. However, soon you may feel that you need an advanced degree to get promotions. Fields such as engineering, computer science, medicine, law, education, higher education and research often require advanced degrees for career progression. Before I started my doctoral studies, I asked myself a thousand times whether I really needed a PhD. I searched for answers on the internet, and everything from blogs in academia and industries to workplace satisfaction measurements gave me the answer that, yes, graduate education is worth it. I am currently experiencing that the answer is correct.

Personal Development

Graduate education often provides students and graduates with opportunities for professional growth, including networking. Graduate schools facilitate times for their graduate students to interact with renowned faculty, professionals, and practitioners in the field, as well as with peers. Building such a network is a great asset for your future career. Usually, graduate degrees are job-oriented, so you can expect hands-on practical experience and field visits and elements that help you acquire skills for your personal development.

Higher Wages

According to the National Center for Educational Statistics (NCES), a person with a master's or higher degree earns 21% more on average than a person with only a bachelor's degree. Advanced degrees are often associated with higher earning potential. When you earn a specialized degree, such as a graduate degree, your field becomes increasingly specialized. Such skills are highly valued in academia and in industry. Also, some job positions require a graduate level qualification for a pay raise.

Independence

Earning a graduate degree can open the door to work that you enjoy more. Let's say you have a bachelor's in chemistry and started working for a pharmaceutical company. You are passionate about chemistry and developing new drugs, and earning a degree in chemistry put you on the right track. But a bachelor's degree alone does not qualify you to develop new drugs; that requires graduate level education, or else you would have to wait for years to gain sufficient experience. A graduate degree offers you a quick path to doing what you really love.

Prestige and Networking

Usually graduate schools are big, well-known universities. For an undergraduate, getting accepted to a prestigious university is extremely hard. Getting accepted to a prestigious graduate school is still competitive, but not as difficult as admitting to an undergraduate program. Graduate education (master's and doctoral degrees) from a reputable institution can elevate your reputation in your field. Advanced educational credentials will make you stand out among your colleagues, and your employer may believe you are more competent. Also, grad schools are bigger institutions which have huge alumni networks. Alumni of prestigious university receive many benefits, including job referral and networking.

Personal Growth

Graduate school is not only a time to gain field-related knowledge, but also a time to grow holistically as a person. During graduate school, you will be trained to think logically, find correct information, and discern facts from misinformation. During your graduate studies, you may gain critical exposure to new technology and gain skills that prepare you for using that technology in your career. As a person who spent seven years in American higher education, I witnessed how higher education quickly adopts new technology and skills and integrates them into the curriculum. Whatever you learn will remain with you forever. The skills, knowledge, and person growth will help you immensely not only in employment, but also more broadly in understanding the world and making educated decisions about your health, wealth, well-being, and personal life.

Share Your Idea Carefully

As you first consider applying for grad school, I would recommend not sharing this dream with those who have not earned a graduate degree. They may hold negative views of higher education or feel threatened by your dreams and criticize you, rather than encouraging your ambitions. Instead, talk to graduate students who are currently successfully pursuing a PhD in your field of interest. Follow YouTube channels and listen to podcasts created by faculty and graduate students. Read books, like this one, that will encourage your dream and guide you through the process of applying to graduate school and earning your graduate qualification.

Choosing to pursue a master's or PhD is a hard decision to make, but you are on the right track. Keep going! The rewards are worth the work.

When To Start Grad School

When is the best time to get a master's or a PhD? The answer is simple: today! You cannot be admitted to a doctoral program overnight, and, once admitted, the program will take time. There is no reason to delay starting the process.

I completed my undergraduate in Sri Lanka when I was 24 and did not start my graduate studies in the United States until I was 29. Many of my undergraduate colleagues started their doctoral studies immediately after earning their undergraduate degree. Since I had never considered pursuing a doctoral degree, and I felt exhausted with academics after my undergraduate studies, I started working after graduation. It took me another four years to understand that I needed a PhD. Looking back, I wish I would have started earlier. So don't be that guy who wanted to start his PhD at the age of 29; start your PhD today, start your master's today. Yet the same applies to the reverse: it is never too late to start. If you are 49 and thinking of starting your PhD, do not worry—you are not too late. Start applying today.

There is much debate around the ideal time to start a master's or PhD. Some say it is best to work in the industry for a while first, others recommend starting in your 30s, and some say it best to start your graduate education immediately after completing your undergraduate degree. While I advocate for starting your graduate studies today, no matter how long ago your undergraduate studies were, I do believe it is best to start and complete your graduate studies early.

There are many advantages of starting your master's or PhD just after your undergraduate studies, but the greatest is your fluency in the academic environment. During undergraduate studies, students are trained to function in the academic environment. They are comfortable in university rhythms, know how to do academic work, and are used to balancing the academic and personal spheres of life. This makes the transition into graduate school smooth. Graduate students coming from the work world can experience a difficult period of transition. I started my master's in chemistry four years after completing my undergraduate degree, and it was challenging at the beginning for me to me redevelop my former academic habits.

What To Study

There are three things that you need to think about before searching for a field of study. The first is your interest. I earned my masters in chemistry and PhD in science education because of my passion: I love chemistry and I love to teach. Think of a field that you love and would not grow tired of. Your passion and personal interest will be significant factors that will help you stay committed to the graduate program until you complete it.

The second thing to consider is your background and previous education. To pursue a PhD in chemistry, you need to have completed a considerable amount of undergraduate or masters level chemistry courses. To start a PhD in mechanical engineering, you may need to have completed some amount of engineering-related courses, as well as gain some amount of related work experience. Examine your transcript(s) and your resume to identify qualification you already have, then use this information to determine what program would be a good fit for you.

The third element to consider is demand. Usually, master's degrees are more job-oriented than PhDs. A master's degree provides many job options, while PhDs may lead to highly specified job opportunities. Even at very large research universities, a physics department may only conduct one PhD program in physics, leaving no options to choose from. Investigate the job placement rate of the doctoral graduates of the particular PhD program you are interested in. Ask how many doctoral graduates in the past three years found their first job within six months after graduation. That answer will indicate how well the program prepares its students for the job market.

After you enroll for a PhD, you still have time to choose your particular field of research. By tracking job markets, you can select a field that will better prepare you for post-graduation employment. For example, currently, many chemistry grad students focus on organic chemistry because of the high job demand in the drug and pharmaceutical manufacturing industry. Similarly, in physics, currently, the semiconductor manufacturing industry drives demand for graduates with experience in material physics and semiconductors.

Do Not Be Too Late

An important, but often overlooked, factor as you consider pursing a PhD is your ability to transfer your credits. Many doctoral schools allow students to transfer master-level course credits to their doctoral programs. Many master's programs allow students to transfer course credits from their undergraduate studies to their master's programs. If you have done grad-level courses (500, 600, and 700-level courses) during your undergraduate studies, those may also be transferrable. Check with your graduate office for the possibility of transferring courses, since the credit transfer process varies from university to university.

In my chemistry master's program, four of us graduated in the same year. All four of us were admitted to doctoral programs in fall of the same year at different universities in the United States. One graduate did not try to transfer course credits. Another one tried diligently, but the university did not allow them to transfer any course credits. The third person was able to transfer eight credits. I was able to transfer 18 credits, making my doctoral degree significantly shorter.

Even if you are a foreign student, you may be able to transfer credits. While transferring foreign credits is harder than transferring local credits, it is still doable, and I personally know a few colleagues who transferred foreign credits to American universities. One of my colleague transferred 30 credits in Engineering from his home country institute to a well-reputed engineering school in US.

It is important to note that undergraduate or master's credits may eventually 'expire,' preventing you from transferring them. By pursuing a PhD or master's sooner, you may increase your chances of transferring credits.

Family And Grad School

Many believe that you need to start your PhD before you get married or have children. This is a common misconception, especially among those without any graduate qualifications. While there may have been some truth to this decades ago, it is no longer true. The university system in the United States is concerned about the well-being of graduate students beyond their education. Graduate studies and family life absolutely can be balanced. I have personally known doctoral students who have navigated family emergencies and even pregnancy during doctoral studies and still successfully completed their graduate studies.

One of my mentors and his wife both were PhD holders living on the West Coast. Their daughter was accepted to a good graduate school on the east coast, but she hesitated to move because she feared losing a serious relationship. My mentor, who is a wise man, encouraged his daughter to choose the graduate school, assuring her that if her boyfriend really loved her, she could have her PhD and her boyfriend in four years. He was correct, and she completed her PhD successfully and continued their relationship, and now they are happily married.

It Is Not That Bad

One challenge that affects more doctoral applicants than master's applicants is the fear of the program. Many people believe that earning a PhD requires extraordinary intelligence and effort. While I agree that it is a life commitment, earning a PhD is not out of reach for regular students. I had the same phobia towards PhDs and master's because I was not a straight-A student. This fear led me to stagnate for four years after completing my undergraduate. The truth is you do not need to be straight A student to start a PhD or a master's. I was not such a student, but I started a full-time master's and completed in two years and then I started a PhD fulltime and finished it successfully in less than four years. If I could do it, you can definitely do it. Earning a graduate degree simply requires a strong will. If you believe in yourself, start it today.

Work Experience

People who argue for gaining work experience before starting master's or doctoral studies highlight that work experience counts on graduate applications. This is true. Graduates with work experience have higher chances of program admittance and typically secure a job more quickly than other graduates after graduation. However, I have also observed that people who begin working after earning their undergraduate degree often settle down, start a family, and become distracted or discouraged from pursuing their grad school dreams. Therefore, I think it is important for those who are considering getting a PhD or a master's to start without delay. If you are an undergraduate in your senior year, start look for good grad schools, prepare your cover letter, communicate with graduate coordinators, and prepare your application.

I am not forgetting my dear readers in their 40s, 50s, and 60s who are planning to apply to doctoral programs. You are not late; start applying now. A PhD at any age can be tremendously rewarding. When I was in the first year of my PhD, I met a person who was in his 60s. As we chatted, I learned that this gentleman was a doctoral student in our grad school. I asked him, "Why? Why earn a PhD at this age? Are you planning to do a job after your graduation?" He explained that he had been working in a renowned art gallery and then retired. He was not looking for a new career; he was just learning for himself. This enlightening answer taught me the value of a PhD.

You are never too late. The best time to start your graduate studies is today.

Reference

- Annual Earnings by Educational Attainment in US (https://nces.ed.gov/programs/coe/indicator/cba/annual-earnings).

CHAPTER 2

SHORTLISTING AND APPLYING

Filling out graduate school applications is a time-consuming task. First, you need to shortlist grad schools that you would prefer to attend. Then preparing for standardized tests, drafting your SOP, requesting recommendation letters, and attending virtual interviews all take a significant amount of time and effort. Do not be intimidated. Applying to grad school is a great investment in your future. Preparing your application package carefully makes you one step closer towards receiving admission to your dream grad school. This chapter will walk you through the timeline and steps of applying to your dream grad school.

When to Start

If you plan to attend grad school, you should start looking for grad schools the summer of the year before you would like to attend (especially for doctoral programs and some competitive master's programs). Most grad school applications are due in fall or early spring, which is why it is better to start your search early. Additionally, application procedures vary from university to university, so early preparation is always a good idea.

Another advantage of early application is alignment with the academic calendar. During your application process, you will need to be in touch with faculty members at the schools you are interested in. Since most academic positions are not paid during the summer (they run on nine or ten month contracts), summer can be a difficult time to receive faculty responses. Additionally, during certain months of the school year, faculty may be so busy with their courseload that they may be slow to respond. If you write to faculty during the beginning of August, faculty are likely to respond quickly, because they are back at work but not yet busy with teaching.

Shortlisting

Some of you may have a clear idea of where to apply. You want to apply to the University of California Berkeley because UC Berkeley conducts the best astrophysics program in the country. Or you plan to apply to Stanford University because you want to be a student of Professor Z, who teaches photochemistry at Stanford University and is a living legend in photochemistry. You may have already formally or informally made contact with the interested parties. In this case, you will likely not have any issue choosing a graduate school.

However, most grad school applicants do not have such strong ties to a particular university. Personally, I did not have an idea initially of where to apply. I just knew I wanted to earn a PhD in science education or chemical education. So, I started my grad school search with science education first. The best place to start your grad school search is the U.S. News website (www.usnews.com), which provides the most reliable, up-to-date grad school rankings. Do not search for best overall university ranking, since the schools with the best undergraduate program rankings do not always have good graduate programs. Search for the best grad school for your desired field.

Let's say you are searching for grad schools with strong physics programs. First, go to the U.S. News website (www.usnews.com), navigate to grad school ranking, and then choose your subject (physics) and search. The website will provide you with a list of graduate schools ranked by the quality of their physics programs. At the time this book chapter was written, the best grad school for physics in the United States was MIT, followed by Stanford, and then Caltech. These rankings are always subject to change.

Likewise, you could search for your subject. Physics is a huge field. If you want to further narrow your search, the U.S. News website provides sub-category rankings as well, which might be useful for your search.

Is US News Enough?

U.S. News graduate school rankings are not everything; there are other factors to consider as you choose your school. Remember that you are not only picking a grad school — you are choosing a location to live for the next four to six years of your life (for doctoral programs). Think about your interests, lifestyle, climate preference, health, family ties, relationship status, marriage, etc.

At the time I was applying for doctoral studies, I was an immigrant who had lived in the United States for two years. I had the freedom to choose a graduate school anywhere in the country. I was looking for a grad school in a diverse, multicultural, low-crime region. I am a brown skinned, south Asian man, so I was concerned about my safety and mental well-being as well. If you are an LGBTQ+ person, in addition to data from U.S. News, you could search grad schools according to the Campus Pride Index (www.campuspride.org), which provides university rankings according to LGBTQ+ friendliness. Do your research and keep searching. If you like country music, look for a good grad school close to a music hub city. If you do not like cold weather, stay away from good grad schools in the upper Midwest and New England. Expand your search and find the best fit.

Curriculum

You need to think beyond university ranking when you choose your dream grad school. When I picked my doctoral school, the U.S. News graduate school ranking had a big influence on my grad school selection. When I graduated with my PhD, those rankings had already changed. So, consider not only the field, but also the subfield.

Assume you are applying to doctoral programs for a chemistry degree. You need to think about which chemistry subfield you prefer. Imagine you want to pursue a PhD in organic chemistry. You need to find out how good the organic chemistry program specifically is at the university you are interested in. You need to identify how many organic chemistry research groups that university has that you could join. Also, it is important to find out the teaching cohort. Are there any renowned faculty? Have recent graduate students been able to find good jobs? Such information should be collected before you apply to any program. U.S. News rankings provide an overall image about the department and the program, but you need to find more information about how well each program fits your interests.

Use Your Contacts

While you are doing your grad school search, don't forget to leverage your personal contacts. If you have a friend pursuing a PhD in science education, and you are also interested in pursuing a PhD in science education, reach out to them. Your friend's university might not be the university for you, but it can still be beneficial to talk with them. If you briefly met a professor at a conference during your undergrad, and she was interested in your poster, reach out to her. Write to her, "Hi Professor K, You met me at the American Chemical Society 2023 conference in Indianapolis. I presented a poster on X. I am interested in applying to your doctoral program at the University of Chicago..." Remember that you may get something if you ask, but if you do not ask, nothing will fall into your lap. If you have a contact at a school, the chances of being admitting to that grad program are greater.

Choose More

Start applying to graduate programs early. You do not need to submit an application to all the grad schools that you shortlist. However, you can start applying to all of them. If you are planning to apply for 10 grad schools, shortlist at least 20 universities. What I am trying to say is, start applying to all the universities, but do not submit an application to all of them, because it will cost you a lot of money. Graduate application fees usually range from $30 to $100. You do not need to spend such money if you are not fully confident of your choice. If the application is free, you can apply without hesitation.

I recommend not applying to your dream grad school first. Start with a safe school and middle to low-priority schools on your list. As you apply to those grad schools, you will learn how the system works and what the graduate schools expect from you. After applying to a few of those grad schools, start applying to your dream grad schools. Take your time to learn what each grad school expects from applicants.

Recruiting Patterns

The American university system is built on recommendations and trends. Selection committees also choose students according to their past experience and current trends. For example, let's say you received your undergraduate degree in biology from Indiana State University (ISU) and many of ISU biology undergrads are admitted to the University of Chicago, Pritzker School of Medicine to study medicine. You will have a greater possibility of being admitted to the Pritzker School of Medicine than any other grad school where no ISU college undergrads are currently studying. Some would not agree with this fact. But the more familiar a grad school is with your background, the better the opportunities you will receive.

I have an interesting story related to this. Two of my colleagues who completed their master's in chemistry with me applied to a high-ranking university in the Midwest. My colleagues knew about this good chemistry doctoral program because, a year before us, one of our alumni was accepted to this grad school. She went on to attend the program and was performing well there. The selection committee was happy to have more grad students from our master's school, so both were accepted. They were invited to visit the school, and the university covered their flight tickets and lodging. They spent a nice weekend at the university, but both of them received better offers from other universities and turned down their first offer. The year after we graduated, two of our junior batch mates applied to the same university, and both were accepted to the program. They were both offered the campus visit, enjoyed a good weekend, but accepted offers somewhere else.

That was the last time that university accepted students from our master's school. The next year I heard some of our master's school colleagues applied to that program, but no one was admitted or even received a virtual interview invitation from that grad school. It was unfortunate and unfair to judge one set of students according to their predecessors. But high-ranking universities receive so many applications that they have to allow trends to shape their decisions.

Write To The Best Person

27

You are not expected to write to faculty prior to applying. However, I followed this method and highly recommend it. Imagine that Princeton is your dream grad school. Prior to submitting your application, go to their website and search for faculty in the department you are interested in. Read their profiles. If you find anyone who is aligned with your research interests, write to that person. Mention your current academic performance, research interests, and your ambition to attend the program. Most likely you will receive a reply from them. Sometimes the reply to such an e-mail is a generic pre-written draft. If you feel the reply is generic, simply send a thank you reply and consider contacting someone else in the department. The more you write, the more likely you will be to find someone who is your best fit.

Sometimes you will receive an exciting e-mail reply from faculty. You will feel the enthusiasm of the responder (the faculty) and their desire to accept you to the program. They may encourage you to apply to the program and ask you for more information about your academics and research experience. They may even invite you for a phone call or zoom call to discuss further. If this happens, you are on the right track.

Faculty are busy people, and during selection time they get even busier. If they offer you a phone or zoom call, that means they are clearly interested in admitting you to the program.

When I was applying to doctoral programs, I had not completed much research. I had not even started writing my thesis. But five program coordinators from five universities wanted to have a zoom meeting with me even before I submitted my application to their programs. One graduate program coordinator introduced me to his current students, past students, and other faculty members. Another university grad program coordinator introduced me to all members of the selection committee and pushed me to contact all of them to increase the chances of being admitted to the program.

Filling Out Applications

Graduate application forms usually ask very basic questions, such as your name, address, and social security number. Provide accurate answers. I have a very long, uncommon name, so I had to be very careful to provide the same name, because most of the time it contradicts clearance and background checks. Each graduate school has a different application form. However, the applications all look very similar to each other with just a few different questions. When they ask your academic and professional qualifications, try to provide answers not for the sake of answering the question, but to elevate the level of your application.

Many prospective grad students ask whether applicants need to mention their ethnicity, race, and other demographic information on their applications. It might be too early to say. The US Supreme Court ended affirmative action in higher education in mid-2023. Educators are closely monitoring the situation, but it might take a few years to determine how this decision affects US higher education. Your demographic information is not as crucial for grad school admission as undergraduate admission, but it is still important. You could provide your demographic information or select "prefer not to say." However, there is evidence that universities try to guess applicants' race and ethnicities (when they indicate "prefer not to say") by using their name, qualifications, and even residential zip codes.

Criminal Records

Getting accepted to graduate school with a criminal record is challenging. However, I wanted to add this section for anybody who needs a second chance. Things may have happened in the past, but everybody has the right to education. Do not lie on applications regarding your criminal record. Instead, disclose all related information. Provide your side of the story in context. You can mention this in your statement of purpose. If your recommenders do not know about your record, inform them. They may write the recommendation accordingly. You can seek advice from law enforcement agencies. Some law enforcement branches have education implementation sections that help recruit individuals with criminal background to different education certifications. You could ask one of them to write one of your letters of recommendation (if you know them well) to provide an image of your good conduct. Draft a strong SOP stating the strengths, skills, experience, and talent you would bring to the school.

Do Not Underestimate

Do not underestimate your value. I was exhausted from my master's academic work and had low mental energy while I was applying to graduate school. But I was surprised and encouraged by the positive responses I received from grad school selection committees. Likewise, remember that you are a very important person to the selection committees. I was not a straight A's student. If I, an average immigrant, could get into graduate school, you can definitely get accepted to your dream grad school. Try hard. You can do it!

Reference

- US News website (www.usnews.com)

- Campus Pride Index (www.campuspride.org)

CHAPTER 3

FUNDING FOR GRAD SCHOOL

Funding is vital for doctoral students. Typically, full-time, in-person doctoral programs at accredited universities offer full funding, while the equivalent master's level programs rarely offer funding in large research universities. Full time master's programs in master's schools may offer full funding. This is just a general principle—funding is not guaranteed. Fully funded programs are hassle free because enrolled students do not have to worry about tuition, living costs, or healthcare. If you are an undergraduate student planning to pursue higher education, I would recommend applying to a doctoral program with internal funding, because you are young and have time. Let's see how internal funding works.

Internal Funding

Of all possible funding sources, internal funding category is the best with regards to availability and benefits. This is the source of funding for most full-time doctoral programs. Still, internal funding does not guarantee full funding upon admission. Let me explain.

Programs at large R-1 level research universities are usually understaffed for the amount of teaching, researching, and laboratory coursework necessary. So, departments offload freshman, and sometimes sophomore, level teaching and laboratory coursework responsibilities to graduate level students. Each year, graduate students are hired in an arrangement called a teaching assistantship (TA). In exchange for teaching a reasonable amount of courses or helping undergraduate students with their coursework, these graduate students are given a monthly or bi-weekly living stipend. Their tuition is paid by the department and their basic health and dental benefits are covered as well.

TA packages vary from university to university, so examine the terms of your benefit package carefully before accepting any offer. Usually, graduate student TAs are considered 50% full time employees (FTE), so they are expected to work 20 hours per week.

Be Crystal Clear

Before joining the program, you have to be crystal clear about funding. By the time you are starting graduate studies, you may have a pile of student debt from your undergraduate studies and possibly your masters. You do not need to increase your student debt further. Additionally, international students are not allowed to work outside of the university. Hence both domestic and international applicants must be crystal clear about funding opportunities before accepting any offers.

Some programs (mostly natural sciences, engineering, medicine, etc.) by default admit doctoral students according to their departmental funding. That does not mean other fields, such as the humanities or business, do not offer funding opportunities for all grad students. Those subjects do have funding opportunities, but the funding may be conditional. Before accepting or rejecting any offer, find out the answers to these questions:

- Will I be funded for the current academic year?

- What is the stipend?

- What benefits (healthcare and vision) would I receive?

- How much are the mandatory fees I need to pay back to the school?

- Will I be a research assistant or a teaching assistant?

- How many years can the program fund me?

- What is the minimum GPA I must maintain to secure my funding?

- Are there any other requirement to maintain to secure my funding?

Most of the answers to these questions will be in your offer letter. You need to track down the rest of the answers before you accept the offer. Reach out to the department contact person, graduate program coordinator, and/or current doctoral and master's students of the program. Clarify all points before you sign your contract and offer letter.

I was fortunate enough to receive full internal funding for my master's and doctoral studies. Sometimes the host department of your intended graduate program cannot offer you funding, but they can connect you with a funding opportunity from another department or a research center. When you request information from the graduate coordinator, you can ask for more details.

RA versus TA

Table 1. RA vs TA comparison

Research Assistant (RA)	Teaching Assistant (TA)
No teaching	More teaching
More research	Less research
No student issues	Student issues

The most common funding opportunities comes as research assistant (RA) and teaching assistant (TA) positions. The advantage of serving as either an RA or

TA is that it will fund your academics (to a certain number of credit per semester) and pay you a stipend.

However, you need to know the differences between an RA position and a TA position. There are pros and cons to both. Teaching assistantships are usually offered by the particular department that you are studying in. TAs teach or co-teach a few classes. Your teaching responsibilities per semester may depend on the program.

In contrast, research assistants do not have any teaching responsibilities. RA positions are offered by research supervisors and funded by their specific research grants. The biggest advantage of being an RA not having any teaching responsibilities. There are no undergraduate problems and no hassle of grading papers; all your time can be spent on research. In my experience, RAs generally receive a slightly higher stipend than TAs, but that could depend on the university. TAs are not funded during summer if the department does not assign any summer teaching responsibilities, meaning they are only paid nine or ten months out of the year. RAs are typically paid all 12 months, as they can research year-round. Some universities maintain a hybrid model: the university pays a TA stipend for nine months, and the research supervisor pays for summer RA work.

Many consider research assistantship positions to be better than teaching assistantships, and I agree with one exception: RAs do not have the opportunity to teach. This may sound like an advantage, but if you plan to go into academia after completing your PhD, this could be a drawback. Most faculty candidates are assessed on their teaching profile and teaching abilities. Some institutions ask their candidates to submit a separate teaching philosophy statement as well.

I taught a variety of classes during my doctoral studies, which really strengthened my job application. You would not believe the bizarre things interview panels ask during prospective faculty interviews! I attended my first faculty interview when I was writing my doctoral thesis, and I was asked about my experience in graduate students supervising. How could I have had grad student supervising experience while I was still a grad student? I was not supposed to have experience mentoring graduate students since I was a graduate student myself, but, because I had supervised a course when one of our faculty members was on sabbatical, I luckily did have some experience and was able to answer the question successfully.

External Funding

If there is no graduate student funding available for you, you can pursue external funding. STEM master's and doctoral applicants and current students can apply for the National Science Foundation (NSF) grant research fellowship program. (This is only available for masters and doctoral programs in STEM and STEM education fields). For more information, go to www.nsf.gov and search "GRFP award." This program offers funding for multiple years. This could be competitive, but each year a considerable number of students receive the award. Receiving this NSF award would also look good on your resume.

In addition to the NSF GRFP award, there are many other opportunities for funding from external sources, including these:

1. National Institutes of Health (NIH)

2. Spencer Foundation

3. GEM Fellowship Program

4. Microsoft Research PhD Fellowship

5. Ford Foundation

6. National Defense Science and Engineering Graduate (NDSEG) Fellowship program

7. Department of Energy, Office of Science

8. Fulbright (international students)

9. Point Foundation (LGBTQIA+ students)

10. The American Association of University movement

Usually, these organizations expect you to apply to a university program first and then submit the scholarship application. Most of these awards consider graduate school applications with pending admission. So prospective students should first apply to the graduate school(s) and then submit their scholarship application. Most of these institutions accept pending grad school applications as well.

The advantage of receiving an external scholarship is that you do not have to work for the university or to the department, allowing you to spend all your time on your graduate education. However, these funding sources typically require you to maintain a certain GPA to keep your scholarship. The other disadvantage is missing out on beneficial teaching and research experience. Teaching and researching time could potentially lead to research publications in peer-reviewed journals. If you do not research and teach, you may have limited opportunities to work on publications. If you receive external funding, make sure that you are engaging in research and other academic and professional activities that strengthen your resume.

Employee Benefits

Some employers offer college benefits. This is common at universities, as university employees are usually eligible to take college classes for free. Even employee spouses are often eligible to take college credits at most educational institutes. When I was pursuing my doctoral studies, I met several university employees (academic and non-academic) who were pursuing a master's or doctoral degree for free. Currently I am employed at a large R-1 level state university. I am allowed to take unlimited amount of college credits, so I take graduate-level courses and learn for personal development for free.

Do not worry if you are not working at a university. Most corporations offer similar college credit benefits to their employees. My university has a long list of corporations and employers (state and private) that offer tuition assistance or reimbursement at our university. If you work at a corporation or an industry, connect with your human resource personnel to ask about such opportunities. Read the requirements that you need to fulfill to pursue graduate-level college credits. Usually, you have to sign a contract when your education is funded by your employer. Read the agreement before you start pursuing your employer-funded grad studies.

Military Tuition Remission

In every graduate application, you have to state whether you or your spouse are on active military duty in the United States. If you are a veteran or an active-duty service member, thank you for your service. You deserve a great graduate education. In all branches of the US defense, there are funding options for graduate education. For example, in the US Army, currently serving personnel can apply to federal tuition assistance (www.nationalguard.com > education-programs > Federal tuition assistance). If you are in the US Airforce, you can apply for military tuition assistance program (www.afpc.af.mil > career management > military tuition assistance program). Also find more details on the Post-9/11 GI Bill (Chapter 33) for graduate level education (www.va.gov > education > about GI bill benefits > post-9/11 GI bill benefits).

These are just a few options to get you started. You can find more details on your defense branch benefits web page. You can also contact your desired university to inquire about active military personnel and veterans scholarships and tuition remission they provide. Your graduate program coordinator might not know about those funding opportunities, since they are offered by the university, not the department. I'd recommend contacting the bursar office of the university or searching their website for more details.

Sustain Without Funding

People who are employed full-time often join doctoral programs and master's programs as part-time students without any internal funding. There are two benefits self-funded students enjoy. The first is that they do not have any teaching responsibilities, which can be burdensome and time-consuming. The other advantage is that doctoral students with assistantships have to maintain a high GPA and good student conduct to keep their assistantship or funding. Self-funding students do not have this pressure. It is common for master's students to manage their work and studies, and there are also part-time doctoral programs available. However, before enrolling in a self-funded graduate program (either master's or doctoral), you must consider your current and future financial situation, even if you plan to apply for student loans.

Student Debt

If a university is not willing to offer you any funding opportunities, you need to look carefully at your financial situation. You do not need to graduate with an extra 100K student debt. By earning a graduate degree, you are hoping to upgrade your life, not unnecessarily risk your financial future, credit score, and long-term happiness. I strongly recommend you do your graduate education without any student debt.

If you have a good job, and your employer fully supports your graduate study endeavors, then you can reasonably self-fund your graduate education. In such a situation, always think about how to reduce your cost of tuition. Apply to state university programs for discounted in-state tuition. If you are applying to a renowned out-of-state university (either state or private), try to compare the value of the tuition you have to pay with the future rewards that your graduate degree will offer you. After you are admitted to the graduate program, you will understand that there are many other important factors that enhance your profile beyond the reputation of the university.

Before you deciding which program to attend, be well aware about fee structures. Also, investigate carefully how each university determines in-state status; being a resident of the state at the moment does not automatically make you an in-state person. I have three graduate level qualifications from three different universities, and each of the three universities held completely different in-state policies. If you do not get an assistantship fellowship or funding, try to apply to scholarships. Often, there are opportunities listed in student portals that few are aware of. If you cannot secure free tuition, at least try to make your tuition costs as small as possible.

Reference

- National Science Foundation - GRFP award (www.nsf.gov)

- US Army scholarships (www.nationalguard.com)

- US Airforce scholarships (www.afpc.af.mil)

- Post-9/11 GI bill scholarships and US Veteran Affairs (www.va.gov)

CHAPTER 4

PREPARING YOUR RESUME

While I use the terms CV and resume interchangeably in this chapter, in the United States, there is a slight difference between a CV and a resume. Most grad schools require an updated CV, which is more focused on academic history than a resume, which typically discusses academic and professional qualifications. Whether a grad school requests a CV or resume, make sure to tailor the document to that particular program of study.

Styling Your Resume

Your graduate application should reflect your academic and professional performance. So, it is important that the appearance of your resume is equally professional. Avoid fancy artistic templates. I would recommend using black, size 12 Times New Roman font. Other standard professional fonts include Arial and Georgia. Check your document carefully for grammatical errors and typos before submitting it.

Read Others' Resumes

I enjoy reading the resumes of highly successful individuals, especially those of successful academics. Many of their accomplishments are summarized on their resume. As you prepare to apply to programs of study, identify faculty you are interested in working with. Their profiles and resumes are typically available on universities' websites. Read a few of those to learn how their academic and professional qualifications are arranged on their resumes. While a grad school applicant like yourself cannot compare your experience and qualifications with those of a tenure track professor at an esteemed university, you can imitate the layout of their resumes. Instead of becoming overwhelmed by their qualifications, simply familiarize yourself with the style and organization of their resumes.

Is there a Required Order to Resumes?

There is no single correct format for successful resumes/CVs. However, there are certain sections of content that must be included, and I can offer general guidelines on organization Start with a header containing your contact information. Then include the following sections: educational background, relevant experience, research experience, publications and presentations, teaching experience, relevant skills, and extracurricular activities. I will elaborate on each of these sections in this chapter.

Educational Background

I recommend beginning with this section with your educational background, since academic qualification are essential for acceptance into a master's or PhD program. Include your bachelor's diploma and master's diploma (if applicable). Consider mentioning your most recent educational qualifications first. For example, if you were applying to a PhD in computer science, and you had completed a master's degree in a related field, you would mention your master's degree first on your CV and then your bachelor's.

You do not need to mention specific courses on your resume, because the graduate school will require transcripts listing all of your classes from your bachelor's and master's degrees. However, you should mention your major and relevant minors. Each entry should state the name of your major, your school, the type of degree that was awarded, the year it was awarded, any relevant minors, your research topic (dissertation), and, if necessary, your research areas. If your major is not relevant to the graduate program but your minor is, emphasize the details of your minor. Always customize your resume to the program you are apply for.

Relevant Experience

On your resume, you can mention your relevant work experience. Beginning with your most recent or most relevant experience, arrange your professional qualifications chronologically. If you worked as a teaching assistant for one year, then you would mention the courses you taught and the labs you supervised along with their dates. You may prioritize new skills on your resume, but all relevant skills, even older ones, are important to mention. For example, imagine you were a freelance science writer during your freshman year, but, due to the overwhelming work load, you quit. If you decided to apply to a physics PhD program, you would want to mention this physics freelance writing experience even though it happened during your first year of college. Always include experiences relevant to the graduate program you are applying to.

On your CV, for each relevant experience, explain briefly what responsibilities you held and how the experience relates to the program. Make sure you convey to the application selection committee what assets you bring to the table. For example, my first job was working as an instructor and a course coordinator for a program. I held both administrative and teaching responsibilities. When applying to a master's program in chemistry, I did not explain much about my administrative responsibilities on my resume, but I did list in detail the subjects that I taught and what level I taught because those were related to chemistry and physics.

Research Experience

If you are an undergraduate student, you may not have much research experience. However, if you have done any level of research in a lab or have been affiliated with a research group, you should mention that on your resume. Some research opportunities are not available to all undergraduates, so, if you earned your undergraduate research position through a competitive process, you should mention that element of competition. Your resume should explain what type of research you have done, describe what kind of affiliation had with the research group, and name your research supervisor.

Publications and Presentations

Remember that you need to mention your publications on your resume. In academia, the highest value is ascribed to peer-reviewed journal publications. If you have any peer-reviewed journal publication citations, include them in your CV in the appropriate referencing style. For example, in the field of education, APA (American Psychological Association) style is the most common, while in chemistry, the preferred referencing method is ACS (American Chemical Society) style. You can cite your publications in your preferred citation method; the most important thing is consistency. Do not cite half of your publications using one citation method and the rest using a different citation method.

McClain, J., Cesljarev, C., Zhong, Q., Rahman, S., Liu, C., Phillips, A., **Ariyaratne, T.**, & Akerson, V. L. (2022). Developing nature of science ideas and orientations at the graduate level: Better late than never. *International Journal on Studies in Education*, 4(2), 155–170. https://doi.org/10.46328/ijonse.82.

In the example above, one of my peer reviewed journal publications is cited in APA 7th edition style. My name in bold. Bolding your name in citations on CVs is a commonly observed practice that helps reviewers more easily recognize your contributions.

How should you arrange your citations? If you have very few citations, arrange them in chronological order. However, especially if you have many citations, I recommend arranging them according to your level of contribution. Publications for which you were the first author would be at the top of your list, followed by publications for which you served as the second author, then the third, etc. This way, anyone who reviews your CV will see your greatest contributions first.

All the other publications are generally considered of lesser value than peer-reviewed journal publications. So, after listing your peer-reviewed publications, list your book chapters, individual conference presentations, round table presentations, talks, and finally post presentations. Mention these clearly but separately; it is an unwritten rule of academic publication hierarchy to not mix different types of publications on CVs.

Other Presentations and Publications

Unique presentations and publications should be highlighted apart from others. For example, if you were applying to a doctoral degree in sustainable development, and last year your essay on sustainable energy was shortlisted to the top 10 sustainable energy essays for the world energy forum essay competition, you would want to mention that accomplishment in a distinct area on your resume. Or, if you were applying to a doctoral studies program in linguistics, and you had presented a Ted Talk on linguistics, you would want to emphasize that on your resume. Such unique presentations and essay publications can make you stand out as an applicant, and your resume provides the best place to spotlight them.

Teaching Experience

Earlier, I mentioned teaching experience in the work experience section of your resume. However, you should mention specifically draw attention to your teaching and tutoring experience. Your resume is not the place to describe your casual tutoring experience. Remember, you should only list professional qualifications. Imagine you tutored your entire frat house in a real analysis mathematics course, and all of them got A's and B's. Good job! But this experience would not make the cut for your CV. Instead, this story could be integrated into your statement of purpose (SOP) or teaching philosophy.

On your resume, communicate your teaching experience clearly to the reviewers. If you tutored multiple courses for multiple levels during your undergraduate and graduate studies, list the title of each course, the level of the course, and the number of students that you taught. Usually, application reviewers understand that 100 level refers to freshman classes, 200 level refers to sophomore, and so on. Highlight in particular any experience you have teaching courses independently.

Other Important Skills

In this section, state your relevant skills and computer application literacy. While you do not need to mention much about each application, you should mention your ability to use important applications for your field. For example, if you are applying to a doctoral or master's program in education, having experience in quantitative tools, such as SPSS and R, and qualitative analysis tools, such as MaxQDA and NVivo, could be an advantage. If you apply to a chemistry doctoral or master's program, experience with ChemDraw could be an added advantage.

It is important to represent yourself and your skills honestly on your resume and application. If you are shortlisted, you will be invited for a zoom interview and possibly a university visit. Your ability to handle computer applications and other skills listed on your resume will be questioned, and any false claims or exaggerations on your resume will likely be detected. It is better to be truthful.

Extracurricular Activities

Mention your extracurricular activities and other important milestones in this section. Again, you do not have to mention all of your extracurricular activities. Always try to make a connection between your qualifications and the program to which you are applying. Put yourself in the shoes of a member of the selection committee and think about how your extracurricular activities might attract their attention. When I applied to my master's degree, I omitted most of my high school level extracurricular activities. However, I did include my role as president of our high school chemistry club, since I was applying to a master's in chemistry.

Customize, Customize, Customize

Make your resume custom-built. You will likely be applying to multiple graduate schools simultaneously, but that does not mean that you should submit the same CV to each program. Instead, tailor your application, including your CV, to each program.

Customizing is a key way to engage reviewers. Members of reviewing panels have to review hundreds of applications. The larger the program, the greater the number of application they receive. During the review process, reviewers shortlist applicants by spending only a few minutes (probably less) glancing at each application. To capture their attention, and maximize your chance of getting shortlisted, you need to clearly demonstrate your suitability for their specific program and strategically present your qualifications, talents, and skills. By tailoring your application for each program, you position yourself to perform better in the review process.

Summary

Even though this chapter discussed the content of a resume point by point, there is no single right way to draft a resume. The two guiding principles are:

1. Express all your relevant qualifications, skills, and experiences on a few pages.

2. Keep the reviewers interested so they engage with your entire document.

3. If you can achieve those two things on your CV or resume, you are on your way to success!

CHAPTER 5

STATEMENT OF PURPOSE

If someone asked me what the most important document is in a graduate school application, I would say it is the statement of purpose (SOP). A strong SOP signals to the application reviewers that you are a qualified candidate. Since this document is so important, I always recommend that applicants allocate two or more weeks to draft and edit it. Use the information in this chapter to compose the first draft of your statement of purpose. Then, set it aside for few days before return to edit it, making sure that it flows and provides a clear image of who you are to the reviewers.

SOP vs. Personal Statement

There are two similar but different documents that graduate schools may require: a personal statement and a statement of purpose (SOP). A personal statement describes you as a person, including your qualifications, skills, and past achievements. A statement of purpose, on the other hand, focuses on your intentions, future goals, and ambitions, along with your qualifications and academic achievements. Every graduate school asks applicants to submit one of these two types of documents. Usually, prospective graduate students apply to multiple universities in one academic year, so be prepared to submit an SOP to some of the schools and a personal statement to others. With these two documents are technically different, in practice, the differences between an SOP and a personal statement are minor.

Do Not Mix

Usually, you will draft one statement of purpose or personal statement and submit it to multiple universities with just a few alterations between each version. This is fine. What is important is submitting exactly what the university requested—either a statement of purpose or a personal statement—and not confusing the two. Even though the differences between SOPs and personal statements are minor, the distinction is critical. When the review panel reads the body of your statement, they may not recognize whether it is an SOP or a personal statement. Do not mention the term "SOP" in a personal statement, and do not mention the term "personal statement" in an SOP.

SOP Guidelines

There is an overwhelming amount of information on the internet about writing a successful personal statement or statement of purpose. It's impossible to read it all. But you should read the SOP or personal statement guidelines of each graduate school you intend to apply to. Furthermore, some departments in the university function like autonomous entities separate from the college or university. In such instances, the review panel may not follow the graduate school's SOP guidelines. To determine whether a particular program follows the university graduate school's guidelines or not, read your particular grad school application form and guidelines. If the program's selection committee enforces the graduate school SOP guidelines, that will be clearly mentioned in the application.

Follow The Links

I have noticed some schools provided links to their graduate school SOP guidelines around the webpage where you are asked to submit your SOP. For example, the University of California Berkeley graduate division provides guidelines on how to write a successful SOP for all UC Berkeley graduate applicants. All UC Berkley graduate program applicants should read these guidelines.

Imagine you were applying to a chemical engineering doctor or program at UC Berkeley. In the process of applying, you discover your application provides direct links to the UC Berkeley graduate division SOP writing page, revealing that you must follow the university grad school SOP writing guidelines. The application even provides clear guidelines and links that would work as a rubric for the selection panel to screen the applicants. In this situation, you would want to read and follow all of these guidelines as you write your SOP.

If an application ever provides SOP guidelines, do not miss any key points. Your application will be reviewed by a group of faculty who have been grading papers for years according to a rubric, and they may grade your SOP methodically according to a rubric.

Organizing Your SOP

Let's start writing your SOP. First, gather all your information, including your CV and transcripts. I prefer referencing hard copies so that I can highlight on them. Write a list of your academic achievements, awards, appraisals. Jot down your passion and motivation. As you examine your updated CV and transcripts, highlight your key achievements and most relevant qualifications for this academic program. You do not need to repeat your transcript and CV in your SOP, but you should draw attention to your exceptional performances and best achievements and talents.

Let's take an example from when I was applying to a master's program in chemistry. I did not have strong research background in chemistry, which could have made it difficult to get accepted into the program with full funding. So, in my SOP, I emphasize other chemistry-related achievements. I highlighted winning first place in a national sustainable development essay competition. I described serving as the president of my high school chemistry club and junior coordinator of the undergraduate university chemistry club. While these positions did not reflect my academic abilities, including them did provide clear evidence of my passion for chemistry.

As another example, for my doctoral studies, I applied to science education programs. I completed a few elective courses on science education during my undergraduate studies, and, as a partial fulfillment of one of the courses, I taught a few science classes in a nearby middle school once a week. I highly emphasized that experience in my SOP, and it worked! I was accepted by multiple R1 level universities, including two universities I had dreamed of attending.

Pull Out Your Ace

Some relevant qualifications and achievements may be hidden in your CV, transcript, and work records. Identify these "aces" by reading your CV and your transcripts carefully before writing your SOP. You may discover valuable information you had previously overlooked. Highlight these in your SOP.

For example, while working fulltime, I also started writing for a science magazine as a freelancer. I was paid little but continued contributing for fun. I never thought the role or experience would be useful to me. However, when I wrote my SOP for my doctoral studies, I explained my experience not only with science research, but also with science outreach. It was a great addition to my SOP. Likewise, identify the ace in your CV according to what program you are apply for.

A Strong Introduction

In your statement of purpose, introduce yourself, who you are, where are you from, why you are choosing to study this, and what your end goal is. Tell the selection committee why you are interested in this position and what qualifies you for this academic program. Remember to make this introduction interesting to read, short, and sweet, since your space is limited. The goal of the introduction is to give your readers a clear, positive mental picture of yourself. Your introduction should be a strong hook encouraging the reviewers to read your entire SOP.

Academic Performance

Talk about your academic performance in a straightforward, appealing way. State the successful completion of your undergraduate studies, and list any medals or awards for academic excellence. Mention any specific electives and compulsory courses you have taken that would make you more suitable for the program. Do not forget to discuss any teaching experience you have, whether serving as a teaching assistant (TA), demonstrator, or even a tutor for colleagues in a professional setting. Having teaching experience offers you an advantage, because many doctoral programs expect graduate students to be teaching assistants. Again, remember this is not a place for a lengthy, boring autobiography. Make everything interesting to read and relevant, while carefully considering the flow of the SOP.

As an example, imagine you were applying to a PhD in statistics. Rather than just mentioning the medal you were awarded for excellence in statistics, you could also describe its significance. You could say you received an award for excellence in statistics after three years with a 3.89 GPA. This hidden information from your transcript makes your accomplishment look even more important.

Or, for example, assume you majored in chemistry, but you minored in mathematics and had a relatively poor GPA in mathematics, which decreased your overall GPA. If you were applying for doctoral studies in chemistry, this story would be important to mention.

Research Experience

Your research experience is a very important factor that strengthens your application, helping you land in the best doctoral school. In your SOP, briefly explain your undergraduate research experience. Your selection committee might not have expertise in your research field or subfield, so explain it in a simple way. On the other hand, do not say that your research is about rocket science and that you cannot explain it to a person who has not completed an undergraduate in rocket science.

Instead, simply convey that you worked on a research project X and obtained Y results. Outreach — including the ability to explain scientific topics to those outside the field — is becoming increasingly important, especially in STEM fields. Your summary of your research experience demonstrates your outreach ability.

Know What You Have Done

I have interviewed many undergraduates for my doctoral research in science education. Sometimes undergraduates were unable to explain their research properly. One time, a senior level chemistry student said she did not do anything during her research except weigh the chemical samples. One junior biochemistry student said he only cleaned labware during his research credit hours. Another student said he ran chromatographic columns and obtained a green color substance, but explained that he did not know anything about the substance he extracted. Students like those would get an A for their honesty, but are unlikely to be accepted at any good graduate school. Make sure that you have a good grasp of your research and are able to explain it to someone who knows the subject to a certain level.

Publications

You do not need to worry about publications. While they can be a great addition to your application, they are not mandatory. Graduate school admission panels do not expect candidates to have high research profiles; they expect applicants to have analytical minds that would thrive in robust research settings. Highlight your passion in research. If you have communicated about your research work (at an international, national, regional, school level), you may mention that.

Supervisor

In your SOP, you could mention the name of your research mentor or supervisor. The professional network is very closely knit in academia, so someone on your selection committee may know your supervisor. For example, if you did research in photochemistry as an undergrad, and now you are applying for doctoral studies in chemistry, there is a good chance the photochemistry faculty in that grad school know your undergraduate supervisor. Selection committees prefer to admit students with known backgrounds, so such references immensely help and may lead to an acceptance letter.

Some universities require a separate letter on your research performance. In such instances, you can provide a brief description about your research in your SOP. Then elaborate on your research expertise in your research performances document.

Anything Else

Do not forget to mention your extracurricular activities. Let's say you are a member of the college cheerleading group. This experience does not directly correlate with your academic accomplishments, but you could add value to your SOP by explaining how you successfully balanced your studies with your extracurricular activities. You could also highlight how extracurricular activities have strengthened your teamworking skills, since collaboration is an integral part of higher education. In your SOP, rather than simply stating facts, aim to connect the dots to defend that you are fully qualified and will bring value to the academic program.

Essay(s) Instead of SOP

While doctoral programs expect their applicants to submit SOPs or personal statements, some master's programs expect their graduate applicants to submit essays. This essay could be one long essay or multiple essays on different topics. Either way, one essay should be obviously related to the program, your professional and academic performance, background, and your contribution to the program. In these essays, you have to concisely explain your talents, performances, background, and future goals in an appealing way. Try to condense the most important points of your SOP into your essay.

You can explain how your personal goals align with the graduate program you are applying to, but do not waste words praising the graduate school or the program. You have a limited number of words to explain your importance to the selection committee. If there are multiple essays to submit, the other topics could be on any topic. Such a topic could be about one of your happiest moments or your critical analysis of a global issue. Thus, the selection committee will analyze your clarity, analytical, and reasoning skills. Be creative and provide essays that the selection committee would love to read.

Diversity and Inclusion

Diversity and inclusion has become a hot debate in higher education. In general, higher education institutions prefer to implement diversity and inclusion actions, but there are mixed feelings among individuals. Some say diversity and inclusion is important, and some say there are other more important things than diversity and inclusion. Faculty with both of these perspectives may be on the selection committee of the graduate program that you are applying, so you need to craft a diversity and inclusion paragraph that is irresistible to both parties. Some universities may ask you to submit a separate diversity and inclusion statement. Be prepared for either scenario.

In your SOP, you need to mention what led you to apply to this program and what has made you who you are. You can talk about adversities you have faced and what has motivated you to become who you are today. For example, if you are an African American girl from a low-income family, your life journey may have been harder than many. Convince the selection committee that you are a person who never gives up. Qualities of determination, courage, and perseverance add value to your profile. Or, if you are a brown-skinned person who identifies as an LGBTQ+ individual, you can mention your journey and hardships you experienced during high school and college. Communicate to the review panel that you have thick skin and can navigate a robust academic environment, and it will be hard for them to turn you down.

You Are Unique

Diversity and inclusion can take place on the grounds of your skin color, race, ethnicity, religion, income, immigration status, location (urban, rural, north, south), disability, etc. If you are a first generation college student, convey how that has made your academic journey unique. If you are from the southern states and applying to a university outside of the South, you could highlight that you are from South. The American South has many prestigious educational institutes, such as LSU, the University of Georgia, and UT Austin, but it is believed that people in the American South have relatively fewer educational opportunities. Or, if you were born and raised in an urban or rural neighborhood with a high poverty rate, mention it. Always connect the dots, expressing how such hardship makes your academic journey unique and how it is relevant to your educational path.

Your Weaknesses

Do I need to share my weaknesses in my SOP? The simple answer is NO. You do not need to mention your weaknesses in your SOP. This document is your defense among hundreds or maybe thousands of other applicants. You are defending yourself in front of a reviewing panel who are eager to dismiss applications. It is not to your advantage to describe what have you could have done better or opportunities you lost during your undergraduates or masters.

79

However, you do need to answer questions that your review panel may ask after reading your application packet. Let's say during your junior year you earned a very low GPA because one of your family members was dying and you had to commute daily and to care for them. This is a very valid explanation for what reviewers will see in your transcript, and it subtly communicates to the review panel that you did not quit your studies even during such hardship. However, if your GPA was negatively affected by a relationship situation, it is better not to state that. The selection committee might think that it could be repeated again during your doctoral studies.

Do Not Contradict

Always connect all the information in your application with the information in your SOP. Try not to contradict yourself. For example, it would be contradictory to describe yourself as goal-oriented in your SOP, but submit a transcript that reveals you changed your major three times and it took you six years to complete your undergraduate degree. Such contradictions undermine the authenticity of your application, causing reviewers to lose their trust in you. To reiterate, the issue is not changing your major or taking extra years to complete an undergraduate degree; the issue is truthful communication. Simply provide accurate information and descriptions in your SOP.

How to End

Write a strong ending for your SOP by make it unique. You could provide a conclusion and state again that you are ready and competent to become a doctoral student in this university. Conclude that, due to x, y, and z reasons, you are well prepared for the graduate program. State that you will bring exceptional skills and knowledge to the program and the school. Convey to the panel that you are the best candidate for the program due to the listed reasons. Tailor your ending as specifically as possible to each university.

Edit Carefully

Read your statement of purpose again and again to make sure there are no grammatical errors or typos, which would reflect poorly on you. Be selective about sharing your SOP, because it contains your personal information, but, if possible, ask your undergraduate supervisor or someone similar to read your SOP. Get their input on its flow and content. There are professional services that review and edit your SOP, personal statements, and other college application documents. You can hire a professional like that who is qualified and experienced to do so.

I would even recommend sending your SOP to a professional editor. I send most of my professional documents to an editor. It is important to make sure your editor will edit without harming the content of your SOP; I always make sure my editor understands what I tried to communicate and will edit my document without tarnishing my ideas. If an editor completely changes your SOP, change your editor or ask your editor to redo their work with proper instructions. It might cost a little money, but you should not submit an SOP that, after editing, sounds like Shakespearean English rather than your voice. Reviewers expect to gain an image of you through your SOP. So, you make sure that your statement of purpose presents your best professional image to the review panel.

CHAPTER 6

OVERCOMING A LOW GPA

Many of you may have this question, which I will address in this chapter. While your GPA does affect your application, having a low GPA does not necessarily mean you cannot get into a good graduate school. In this chapter, I will offer strategies for overcoming a low GPA to get into the grad school of your dreams. To be clear, if you have a stellar 4.00 undergraduate GPA, this chapter is not for you; this chapter is meant for those who are worried that a low GPA may limit their graduate school ambitions.

You may find yourself in this position for a variety of reasons. If you are close to graduating from an undergraduate program, changing your GPA is very difficult. If you have already graduated, you cannot change your undergraduate GPA. What constitutes a "low" GPA is somewhat ambiguous. One person might consider a score below 3.25 out of 4.0 a low GPA, while another might consider anything less than a 3.0 out of 4.0 a low GPA. Let's say below 3.25 as a low GPA (this is very subjective). Regardless of how you define a low GPA, having a low GPA is not the end of the world. I have known many people with low GPAs who were admitted to good grad programs. The key is having substitutes to compensate for your low GPA.

Quantity versus Quality

GPA, or grade point average, is a single number value with two or three decimal points (usually ranging 0 – 4). While that number quantifies the grades you earn in your classes, it does not quantify the quality or rigor of what you studied. Therefore, emphasizing the rigor of classes you have taken is the first way to overcome a low GPA in the graduate school application process.

Imagine two students majoring in chemistry. One has a higher GPA and the other has a lower GPA. The one with the higher GPA only completed compulsory courses in chemistry and took easy electives from different departments across the campus. In contrast, the second student with the lower GPA not only completed all compulsory chemistry courses, but also took challenging chemistry electives, including courses such as organic chemistry II, medical chemistry, and molecular spectroscopy. Additionally, the second student completed a minor in biochemistry. In such a situation, despite her lower GPA, the second person would be more eligible for a graduate program in chemistry than the first person.

You will have to send your transcript with your grad school applications, revealing your low course grades. However, you can craft your statement of purpose (SOP) to emphasize how your desire to study chemistry led you to enroll in all chemistry courses, including harder ones, which reduced your GPA, but that you learned a lot. Highlighting your valuable experiences and your knowledge and skills demonstrates to the application reviewers that, despite your lower GPA, you will be a great asset to the grad school.

Valid Reasons

One way to get admitted to a good grad school with a low GPA is by convincing the selection committee that your GPA does not accurately reflect you and your academic capacity. Explain in your application any extenuating circumstances or reasons for your low GPA. For example, you might have experienced personal issues during your undergraduate studies. Perhaps a family member was sick, causing poor academic performance during your junior year. Your low freshman year GPA could be attributed to challenges adjusting to college life. Or perhaps, you were struggling with your health condition while managing your studies.

These are valid reasons for a low GPA, and it is good to admit mistakes you made earlier in your academic career. However, it is key to convince the committee that you are now a dedicated and responsible adult capable of handling the rigors of a graduate program. It does not reflect well on the graduate school for students to drop out mid-program, so the selection committee wants to make sure that applicants are well-suited for the program.

Good Standardized Test Scores

Standardized test scores are another way to mask your low undergraduate GPA and prove that you are now well prepared for graduate studies. The best example is the GRE (Graduate Record Exam), a graduate school preparedness test, or the similar GMAT, a standardized test for business school admission, LSAT for law and MCAT for medicine. While many criticize standardized tests' content, the Education Testing Service (ETS), which develops the exams, continuously proves that the GRE and other standardized tests reflect applicants' graduate school preparedness.

Unlike other standardized tests, the GRE provides scores as percentiles. For example, if you earn a quantitative reasoning score of 80th percentile, that means your score is ahead of 80 percent of the exam takers. That information provides the selection committee with important information about your suitability for their program. Additionally, the GRE provides the opportunity to demonstrate your knowledge of specific subjects. If you are applying to a grad school for subjects like mathematics, physics, or psychology, and you think your undergraduate GPA is low, you can take a relevant GRE subject test. A high GRE subject score can help you to cover up your poor GPA score to a certain extent. However, getting high GRE scores does not fully mask your poor undergraduate GPA" is grammatically correct.

Please note that standardized tests and GPAs are two distinct metrics. A GPA is a score that you acquire after completing close to 120 course credits, whereas most standardized tests are only a couple of hours long. The information provided by these two datasets differs. Selection committees typically place higher importance on your undergraduate GPA than on your standardized test results. However, this does not imply that you cannot gain admission to your desired graduate school because of a poor undergraduate GPA. You can demonstrate that your undergraduate GPA does not accurately reflect your academic preparedness for graduate school with evidence.

Related Career Experience

Your personal statement offers space to demonstrate your readiness and eligibility for a graduate program based on relevant career experience. For example, you may have gotten a low GPA in your electrical engineering undergraduate degree, but now you are working at a power distribution company, and you handle a lot of job duties related to electrical engineering. In your personal statement, you could describe this experience and explain how it makes you a strong grad school candidate.

This is a common practice among master's level applicants. Since many master's level programs are career-oriented programs, having a good career background can give you good leverage on your application. While less common among doctoral level applicants, it is still appropriate to mention career experience if it is very relevant to the doctoral field to which you are applying. For example, if you were applying to a doctoral program in chemistry, and you had worked as a junior level scientist at a well-known drug manufacturing company for five years, you would want to convince the selection committee that you gained valuable knowledge from this work experience.

However, as you describe you career experience on your application, do not downplay your undergraduate academic experience. Academic experience and accomplishments are still considered more valuable than career experience on graduate school applications, since applications are reviewed by individuals in academia.

Bridging Programs

Another way to increase your chances of being admitted to a graduate school despite a low undergraduate GPA is by completing a bridging program. Imagine that you are thinking of applying to a doctoral program in economics, but you earned a poor GPA during your undergraduate economics degree. You could do a one or two year master's program in economics prior applying to a doctoral program in economics. Earning a better GPA in this program would prove to the selection committee that have become a better student and are prepared for PhD studies.

A bridge program does not have to be a master's degree. You could do a graduate certificate program or a complete a non-credit certificate towards your program. Open source MOOCs (Massive Open Online Courses) are also great way to learn at very low to no cost. Aspiring grad school applicants can take MOOCs via Coursera (www.coursera.org) or EdX (www.edx.org) and receive good grades for related subjects, improving the strength of their application. For example, if you wanted to be accepted to a physics doctoral program at Princeton, one way to increase your chances would be to take some of the physics open source courses conducted by Princeton in Coursera.

Additionally, if you are planning of doing a field change, I also recommend completing a bridging program. Imagine that you studied English for your bachelor's degree, and now you want to pursue a PhD or a master's in informatics. It would be a good idea to pursue graduate level courses in informatics and earn a high GPA prior to applying for PhD or master's programs to prove your preparedness.

Strong Recommendation Letters

Strong recommendation letters can elevate a graduate application. Please note that this means strong recommendation letters, not recommendations from strong and powerful individuals. Assume, for example, that you did an excellent job during your undergraduate capstone project and your supervisor was impressed. He suggested you apply for grad school and was willing to give you a recommendation letter. This recommendation letter would be valuable as your capstone project supervisor would describe not only your strengths, skills, and abilities but also your learnability.

Graduate applications require at least three recommendation letters, so you should find at least three individuals who can provide you with strong recommendations. Recommendation letters play a more significant role in doctoral programs than master's programs, since doctoral candidates must work under a supervisor. Supervisors prefer to know applicants' trainability, how quickly they learn, and how well they will likely work with a supervisor.

Research Exposure and Publications

During the time that I was applying for my PhD, I talked with a colleague who had completed his undergraduate degree with me and who was also applying for doctoral studies. He did not have good undergraduate GPA, and he did not score well on the

GRE, but he was able to find a good PhD school. After earning his undergraduate degree, he started a part-time master's program. During his master's, he conducted research with his supervisor, and they were able to publish many papers in well-known, peer-reviewed journals. Because of these publications, even though he did not have any other qualifications, he was accepted to a good doctoral program in the United States. Publications are another vital part in your graduate application. If you have good journal publication citations, that elevate your grad school application.

Internships and Volunteer Work

Doing volunteer work is not a common practice among graduate school applicants, but it is still worth mentioning here. I have met a few people who followed this path and were admitted to grad school. One person who I met had a master's and undergraduate degree in physics, and he was wanted to pursue doctoral studies in physics. However, he could not leave the town because of family ties. So, he had limited graduate school options and had to find a doctoral program within a commutable distance.

He wrote to several faculty members at nearby schools who were conducting research in his field of interest. Eventually, one faculty member asked him to come and volunteer in his lab a few days a week. He worked well there, and, while he was volunteering, one of his research work published in a peer review journal. After a few months of volunteering without a pay, he was offered a research assistant position by his supervisor and was admitted to the PhD program in that university.

This is one successful story, and there could be many—including yours. If you have a strong will, nothing can stop you on your grad school journey.

Summary

When I started applying for graduate school, I was a little worried about my undergraduate GPA. I was sure that my skills and talents were reflected well in my transcript. However, after my undergraduate degree, I completed a master's degree (which was not related to my target grad studies field), and I started another graduate diploma in chemistry. I scored well on those diplomas, so, even though these certificates and transcripts were not requested, I sent copies of the transcripts to my desired schools to prove that I was well prepared to be a doctoral student. I received admission from three schools with funding.

So, stop worrying about your undergraduate GPA! The past is past, and you need to face the future. Many recent undergraduates believe that a poor undergraduate GPA is a permanent scar, but that's not true. Graduate application reviewers understand that people change. The only thing you have to do is use solid evidence to convince the selection committee that you are capable of pursuing grad studies and that you are the right fit for their robust grad program. With the tools in this chapter, you can overcome your low GPA and attend your dream grad school.

References

- Coursera (www.coursera.org)
- Edx (www.edx.org)

CHAPTER 7

RECOMMENDATION LETTERS

A recommendation letter is a critical component of your doctoral application packet. A recommendation letter reflects a candidate's grad school preparedness, teachability, and willingness to work under those with higher authority. While grad students need to be independent, they also should be flexible enough to listen to advice and guidance from their supervisor and other faculty.

Many applicants question the importance of recommendation letters. I felt uncertain about recommendation letters when I was applying to graduate schools. Yet they are critical. Any grad applicant can boast about themselves in their SOP; recommendation letters provide greater assurance that an applicant is prepared for grad school (or not). Recommendation letters are confidential documents, meaning that applicants do not know what is written in them. While you have no control over what the recommenders write, you can pick the people who write the letters. So, pick your recommenders wisely.

Who Should Write Your Recommendation Letters?

For grad school applications, there are usually no restrictions on who can write recommendation letters. However, you have to pick your recommenders carefully. Ideally, your recommenders will able to recommend you whole heartedly with specific evidence demonstrating that you are a good fit for the graduate program. These people should have known you for a considerable amount of time in a professional capacity. The author of each recommendation letter is required to explain their relationship with the person for whom they are writing the letter.

If you have recently finished your undergraduate studies, the best people to write your recommendation letters are your university professors. If you have conducted any research, seek a recommendation letter from your research supervisor. Whenever possible, try to obtain letters of recommendation from people in the same or similar field to which you are applying. If you are currently completing your undergraduate or master's degree, cultivate good, professional connections with at least three of your professors who will be able to write recommendation letters for you. Usually, universities ask for three professional recommendation letters, but that could vary.

Remember this: if you did not have a positive professional relationship with an individual or program, do not ask them for a recommendation letter. For example, if you were going to apply for a doctoral program in mechanical engineering, but you had complicated relationship with your undergraduate mechanical engineering department and faculty, you would not want to ask them for a recommendation letter and risk your graduate application. Only ask for a recommendation letter from those who can confidently endorse you.

Do Not Take Risks

I should share a personal experience with this. I applied to a chemistry master's program four years after I completed my undergraduate degree. By the time I was applying, there was no one at my undergraduate institute from whom I could confidently ask for a recommendation letter, even though I studied chemistry and physics there. After completing my undergraduate degree, I pursued a program to fulfill my credit requirements. There was a faculty member who was not very friendly, but I enjoyed his subject, scored well in the class, and actively attended lectures. So, I decided to ask him for a recommendation letter. He was not very happy about writing me a recommendation letter but agreed to write one.

A few weeks later I received notifications from all the universities to which I was applying that they had received my recommendation letter from this person. He e-mailed me a copy of the recommendation letter he submitted to all the universities, even though I did not ask to see it. It was not a recommendation letter, but a disapproval letter! I could not think of any reason why this person would do such thing to me. He had already sent this terrible letter to all the universities; there was no way to un-do the catastrophe.

So, I would strongly recommend staying away from such toxic people. It does not matter if your recommender has received a Nobel Prize or a Field medal—if you are not 100% confident that the person will write positive things about you, do not ask them for a letter. If you are unsure, ask the person directly whether they will write a positive recommendation letter. If they say that they are happy to write your recommendation letter, go for it. If they are hesitant or unwilling, respect their decision and move on to your second choice.

Remember – Review panels know that those who provide recommendation letters generally write positive things about candidates. Reviewers search through letters of recommendation to find anything negative that recommenders have written about applicants and highlight those negative points.

Academia or Corporate Sector

When I was applying to master's programs, I had been working at a university as a lecturer for four years. I asked for a recommendation letter from my supervisor at my workplace. Even though he did not know my academic performance, he knew my work ethics and teaching abilities. He was also a faculty member, so he was eligible to provide me with a good recommendation letter. I could trust him to provide a strong letter of recommendation over a professor who barely remembered me from my undergraduate studies.

A great recommendation letter highlights your academic skills, talents, and teachability and will identify you as a good fit for the graduate program. I have already explained the dangers of bad recommendation letters, which, unfortunately, are not rare. But there is another category of recommendation letters, too, that I call "generic recommendation letters." These do not say anything great, but neither do they say anything bad about you. If you do not have any one who could provide you with a strong recommendation letter, finding someone willing to write a generic recommendation letter is not a bad option. A generic recommendation letter is better than a disastrous letter, like the one I mentioned earlier.

How To Request A Recommendation

If you are planning to apply to a doctoral program, think of at least three to four potential recommenders and ask whether they would be willing to provide you with a recommendation letter. If you can find five people who agree to provide good recommendations, that is awesome. Plan to provide your recommendation writers with at least one month to submit their letters. They are busy with their academic work, and you are asking for additional work that they are not paid for. During the doctoral application season, your recommenders might receive multiple requests from many other applicants like you, so do not wait until the last moment.

Use The Correct Email

I have submitted multiple applications for grad schools, once for my master's and once for my PhD. I sent all my recommendation letter requests electronically. Physical recommendation letters are very rarely acceptable nowadays. While I was teaching, I had to send recommendation letters for my undergraduate students, and everything was done electronically. All you have to do is enter your recommenders' e-mail addresses in your application portal, and a recommendation request will be sent to the recommender automatically. Make sure to send the request to their official email address, since anyone can create a Gmail or Yahoo email account and impersonate a faculty member. If your recommender is from corporation or government agency, request their official email address rather their personal email address.

Make It Confidential

You have the ability to make the recommendation letter confidential or visible to you (non-confidential). Generally, recommendation letters are sent confidentially. Your recommenders might not be comfortable showing their letter to you, so I recommend making it confidential.

Remember - Application reviewers may not give the same weight to the non-confidential recommendation letters as to confidential letters. Also, your recommenders may not be as willing to give you a recommendation letter if it is nonconfidential. So, the best thing to do is to make your recommendation letters confidential. You make this choice when you provide each recommender's details to the grad application portal, and your recommender will also be informed of the status of the letter (confidential or not).

What Information Is Needed

A good recommender needs a thorough understanding of who you are. So, when someone agrees to write a recommendation letter for you, consider sending them a small packet of information to help them draft your recommendation letter. If you have taken any classes from this professor, remind them of those classes (including course number, course title, and year), as well as the grades you earned. Attaching a transcript is not a bad idea if you are confident with your overall grades and fully confident in your recommender. If you have done any internships, volunteering, or any other relevant training with this recommender, mention those as well.

If you have received any awards, honors, or anything related to your prospective field of study, you may provide information about that. You do not have to mention irrelevant details, like being voted homecoming queen. If you feel something is relevant, state it in a proper and concise way. It is also advisable to send a copy of your updated resume to your recommender. If you have already finalized the list of graduate schools to which you are applying, send it with the application due dates.

Drafting A Recommendation

Recommenders may ask you to draft the skeleton of the recommendation letter. Sometimes they may ask for additional information to be included in your recommendation letter. This happened to me few times, so it might happen to you as well. It does not mean that your recommenders are asking you to write your own recommendation letter. You can write a small blurb about yourself and why you think you would be a good candidate for graduate school. Provide solid information that is relevant to your recommender and to the grad program. For example, do not write about being the high school valedictorian if your recommender is your senior-year quantum physics professor. Instead, remind your professor about how faithfully you attended her class and how you scored the highest in your exam.

You can use details to elevate your letter of recommendation. For example, instead of simply stating, "Jenna scored the highest in her class for her quantum mechanics course," write, "Jenna is a very attentive student; she scored the highest grade in her class among 56 students in a three credit senior level quantum mechanics course." Your physics professor might not remember that microlevel information – it's your job to remind them. Do not provide any false information. Your information might still accessible to your professor. Be honest and it will be rewarded!

Follow Up

Even though you are not allowed to read a confidential recommendation letter, you can see the status of these letters. Usually, most university application systems are designed to send you a notification when a recommender submits a letter. Do not forget that unless the required number of recommendation letter are submitted, your application is not complete and will not be sent. So, keep an eye on the status of each of your grad school applications. Prepare an excel sheet (mentioned in grad school timeline chapter) with each grad application its corresponding due date. If a recommender has not submitted their letter within a month of being contacted, and the due date is approaching, you can send your recommender a reminder. If you have tried to communicate with your recommender, but they are unresponsive, contact the graduate coordinator of the grad school to which you are applying. They may have an alternate solution for you.

Red Flag

There are instances in which a graduate school selection committee is keen to admit a candidate to their program but asks the candidate for an additional recommendation letter. If you find yourself in this situation, it may be a red flag notifying you that one of your recommenders submitted a less-than-ideal recommendation letter. The graduate application reviewers are asking for a new recommendation letter to replace the bad one. If you plan to apply to any other universities, try to identify and avoid that recommender. I know it is difficult to suspect one of your trusted recommenders of being a black sheep. However, this kind of incident happens in the academia and could happen to you.

Thank Your Recommenders

Once all your recommendation letters have been submitted, do not forget to thank your recommenders. They have played a significant role in your application process. Also, when you receive and accept an offer for a graduate program, you should inform your recommenders and thank them again. This is not necessary, but most of your recommenders support you and would love to hear about your progress. Your recommenders continue to be your contact point to students and faculty of your new graduate school, for, while the American higher education system is immense, the faculty and graduate student communities are tightly knit within their field of expertise.

CHAPTER 8

GRE

The GRE, or Graduate Record Exam, is the most widely accepted standardized test for graduate school. It is considered a measurement of a candidate's graduate education preparedness. This chapter provides you with the basics you should know before taking the GRE. Like with other standardized tests, graduate schools do not provide a GRE cut-off mark for admission. However, if you have a low undergraduate GPA (Grade Point Average), or you are making a subject change, you should strive to perform well on this exam. In 2023, the GRE underwent many changes which appeared to benefit exam takers. Specific GRE testing information is always subject to change, so you can read the most up-to-date exam instructions on the testing agency's website (www.ets.org).

GRE Exam Structure

There are two main types of GRE exams: the general GRE and GRE subject tests. The general exam is becoming more popular than GRE subject tests among test takers and graduate schools. Let's talk about the general GRE first. It is composed of three categories and five sections.

Table 2.

Test sections, questions, and timing (Since 2023)

Category	Segments and questions	Time allocation
Analytical Writing (One section)	One task	30 minutes
Verbal Reasoning (2 sections)	Section 1 – 12 questions	18 minutes
	Section 2 – 15 questions	23 minutes
Quantitative Reasoning (Two sections)	Section 1 – 12 questions	21 minutes
	Section 2 – 15	26 minutes

	questions	

1. Analytical writing

There is one 30 minutes analytical writing section. Test takers are given a situation to analyze and must provide an analytical statement. To perform well on this section, you should be able to convey complex ideas simply and clearly using standard written English.

2. Quantitative reasoning

This segment still has two sections, but, unlike before, it now has fewer questions in each section. The first section has 12 questions, and 21 minutes are provided to answer them. In the second section, 15 questions need to be answered in 26 minutes. This is a math test that assesses your mathematical problem-solving ability. Usually, this test consists of basic arithmetic, algebra, geometry, and data analysis.

3. Verbal Reasoning

Since 2023, the verbal reasoning part has consisted of two sections. In the first section, 12 questions need to be answered in 18 minutes. The second section has 15 questions, and 23 minutes are provided to answer them.

This is the language assessment part of the exam. It examines perspectives, multi-levels of meanings, and summarized texts, as well as test takers' understanding of individual words, sentences, and concepts.

When I took the GRE, it was close to a four hour long exam. However, after the 2023 update, the entire exam was shortened to two hours. I think shortening the exam benefits exam takers, since longer exams exhaust exam takers and cause poor scores.

GRE Subject Tests

ETS, the company that administers the GRE, currently offers mathematics, physics, and psychology subject tests. It discontinued the chemistry subject test in 2023. Each of these subject tests has its own curriculum and content. If you visit the ETS website (www.ets.org), you can find more information about the subject tests. Applying to a grad school to study one of those subjects (mathematics, physics, or psychology) does not necessarily mean you have to take the subject test over the general test. I was admitted to graduate school during the time ETS offered the chemistry GRE subject test. However, none of the schools I applied to required me to take the chemistry subject test, so I only took the general GRE.

Subject or General GRE

Doctoral applicants in mathematics, physics, and psychology may wonder which GRE exam to take. It all depends on what the universities you are applying to require. If your target graduate school asks for a subject GRE test, you should take the subject test. However, most universities accept—or require—GRE general scores and consider subject tests optional. Go to the website of any university graduate school you expect to apply to. Under the admission requirements page, you can find which GRE tests that they accept. If any graduate program states that GRE general exam results are required, and GRE subject exam results are optional, then you must take the GRE general test. You may or may not submit the subject GRE exam results.

It is always better to take GRE general exam. Something is better than nothing. But there are doctoral programs (even at Ivy League schools) that do not require applicants to take the GRE (neither subject test nor the general exam). During the COVID pandemic, many grad schools waived GRE and standardized test requirements. Now they are reinstating GRE requirements for grad school applicants.

GRE subject tests are not as readily available as the general GRE test. Many universities make subject tests optional. However, some universities allow students to bypass prerequisite classes if they have completed a GRE subject test and earned a certain score. This often happens for those admitted to a doctoral program. You will be asked to sit an admission test or multiple tests provided by the department. If you do not earn certain scores, you may have to take undergraduate prerequisite classes. Applicants to graduate programs in mathematics, physics, and psychology may contact their department to ask whether there is a possibility of waiving those departmental exams with GRE subject tests. If there is a mechanism of waiving the admission tests with GRE subject test scores, you should take the GRE subject test.

GRE Scores

- Verbal reasoning scores vary from 130 to 170.

- Quantitative reasoning scores vary from 130 to 170.

- Analytical writing scores vary from zero to six on a half point scale (scores could be 6, 5.5, 5.0, etc.). If the question was not answered, the candidate receives no score (NS).

What Score Is Required

It is hard to tell what is a "good" or "bad" score for the GRE. The GRE is a required component of most graduate applications, but most universities are reluctant reveal their cutoff GRE score. One time I had a discussion with my supervisor about how GRE requirements affect applications. She said they do not have a cutoff GRE score. Instead, she said that they checked the applicants' scores' percentiles. She has chaired multiple grad application selection committees. Actually, if you take a GRE result sheet, it provides your score and percentile for quantitative and analytical reasoning. That provides a good image of an individual candidate's score alongside the other exam takers' scores. Prospective candidates should try to score their best in all GRE components. However, engineering, computer science, chemistry, and most STEM field graduate programs expect higher quantitative reasoning scores, while humanities and social sciences graduate programs expect higher verbal reasoning scores from their graduate applicants.

GRE Preparation

GRE preparation needs to be done ahead of time form many reasons. First, it takes time to prepare for the exam. Second, you cannot take GRE exams one after the other; once you have taken the exam, you need to wait 21 days before taking the exam again. And you can only take the exam five times within a period of 12 months. Additionally, the exam costs $220. As you pay a significant amount of money per sitting, you need to make sure you score your required score on your first or second attempt.

There are multiple GRE practice kits available on the market. You could buy one to prepare. Upon registering for the exam, you can also download two free ETS practice tests. The exam structure is very similar to these practice tests. In fact, I have not found any commercially available practice guides more similar to the actual GRE test than the one provided by ETS. Identify which section (verbal or quantitative) you are stronger in and which one you need more support in, and study accordingly. I highly recommend you to do both ETS practice tests the day before the exam day.

GPA Over GRE

The beginning of the chapter stated that if you have a poor undergraduate GPA, scoring well on the GRE is crucial. However, your undergraduate GPA sends a stronger message to your selection committee than your GRE score. Your GPA is a score earned over four years of hard work. You had to take at least 120 course credits to earn your GPA. The GRE is now a two hour long (or maybe even shorter) exam. While obtaining a good GRE score is crucial for applicants with a poor undergraduate GPA, applicants with a poor undergraduate GPA should address their reasons for that poor undergraduate GPA (if there are any) in the application. Refer to more information on this in SOP chapter.

Do Not Make Any Mistakes

Not all smart students are the best test takers. Not all the best test takers are the best students. Educators and test developers are well aware of this phenomenon. However, for centuries exams have been considered the best possible way to assess students in formal education, and no other method has replaced the role of exams in student assessment. Smart students who are not good exam takers—you have to tackle this. If you believe you do not perform well during exams in general, prepare well for the GRE. Understand how you can overcome exam phobia and stress. If you believe one standardized test works better than the other, you can choose (if you can choose GMAT and LSAT instead GRE).

The GRE is not designed to measure all your mathematical and English language knowledge. The quantitative reasoning section usually comes from high school and middle school level mathematics. Instead, the GRE assesses your ability to answer rational questions in a small period of time. So do not make silly mistake when answering the question. Even if you solve a math problem correctly, you will only receive credit if you select the correct answer on the screen. Imagine you found the answer to a problem is 2x. You might click x as the correct answer on the screen because all the answers look similar. Working out the correct answer on the piece of paper and choosing the correct answer on the screen are also a part of the process.

Registration Fee Reduction And ID

You can go to the ETS website (www.ets.org), create an online account, and register for the exam. You can find the exam centers and availability dates in your profile. Make sure to add your information (your name) exactly as it appears on your photo ID. You can use a government issued photo ID. Please read the instructions in your admission letter and on the ETS website for more details. International applicants should check country specific ID requirement in the website. In some countries, ETS only accepts valid passports. You need to confirm all this information before you attend the exam. Different countries have different fee structures (for example China).

If you feel that you have financial hardship, unemployed, or you identify as an individual of an underrepresented group in the US, you can request a fee reduction. These privileges are mostly available to U.S. citizens and permanent residents. If you are an international applicant, you may contact your local ETS service provider for such privileges, or you could directly contact ETS. Each graduate school in the United States has an ETS code. You need to know your grad school code to send your GRE transcripts. After the completion of the exam, you have the opportunity to send your GRE scores to four graduate schools for free. Try to remember 4 schools' ETS codes or the exact names of the Graduate School that you have applied to or plan to apply to. Or else carefully choose the university you are going to apply to.

Table 3.

Universities with GRE codes

ETS Code	The University
1832	The University of Chicago
1851	The University of Illinois - Chicago
1836	University of Illinois - Urbana Champaign
1787	University of Illinois -

	Springfield

Let's take these four institutions. The names of these universities are very similar, but they are completely different institutions. If you want to apply to the University of Chicago law school, but you send your GRE scores to the University of Illinois Chicago, you cannot get it back. If you need to send an additional copy to another institution, you have to pay extra, so please apply carefully.

An increasing number of law schools and business schools have started accepting GRE exam scores instead of LSAT and GMAT scores respectively. You can find the accepted Law school and Business School list on ETS website (www.ets.org), or you can check directly with the graduate school to which you plan to apply. However, that does not mean that taking the GRE over the LSAT, or taking the GMAT over the MCAT, is beneficial. Follow your desired dream grad school admission requirements carefully. I conducted a long survey of the top business schools' and law schools' admission requirements in the US. Many of them state that they accept both the GMAT and the GRE or the LSAT and the GRE. However, if all the other candidates who applied to one business school submit a GMAT except you, or few, including you, applied with the GRE, that might give you a disadvantage. Hence if you are applying to a competitive business school or a law school, try to contact your grad school advisor to get more information. I have decided to provide some information on the GMAT, LSAT, and MCAT exams in this book, because I know some of you are seeking to attend business school, law school, or medical school.

References

• Education Testing Service (www.ets.org).

CHAPTER 9

GMAT, LSAT AND MCAT

If you are planning to apply to medical school or law school, the application instructions are extremely field-specific and program-specific. A book could be written just on law school admission or medical school admission. However, I am writing about field-specific standardized tests, because there is an overlap on these standardized tests. As we discussed in the previous chapter, sometimes you may be able to replace the GMAT and LSAT with the GRE. On the other hand, some engineering management graduate programs and information technology management graduate programs may ask you to provide GMAT scores instead of GRE scores. Also, you need to identify which standardized test fits your requirements and which test you may score better on. Among the readers of this book, there might be many who graduated with an undergraduate degree in something else, but have a nurtured a life-long dream of pursuing an MBA, for example. This chapter is for all of you. Even if you do not know what the GMAT, LSAT, and MCAT are, this section will still help you.

GMAT (Graduate Management Admission Test)

The GMAT is specifically designed for post-graduate level business school admission in North America. It is also the most common standardized test for post-graduate level business schools globally. Most competitive MBA programs require the GMAT for admission. Additionally, some doctoral programs in business and management, graduate level engineering management programs, and some information technology graduate programs require GMAT scores. So, candidates should check their specific graduate school requirements (even in engineering and computing schools) to determine whether they need to take the GRE or GMAT. If the university states that they accept both, find out which the selection committee prefers and which exam you might score better on.

As you decide which exam to take, you need to think about exam structure. If you think you can score better on the GMAT over the GRE, I think doing the GMAT is a wise idea. Earlier, I mentioned how I chose to take IELTS over the TOEFL exam, even though TOEFL is the most accepted language proficiency test in the USA. For me, the decision was simple. The IELTS exam was relatively cheaper, I was comfortable with the exam structure, and I prefer pencil and paper test over computer-based exams. So, I choose IELTS over TOEFL.

The GMAT assesses the analytical writing, quantitative reasoning, verbal reasoning, and integrated reasoning skills of candidates. The GMAT is a standardized test designed to assess graduate level management education preparedness. Unlike the GRE, the GMAT is specifically designed for business and management-related graduate programs. If you have decided to pursue a graduate degree in a related field, you should think about taking the GMAT instead of the

GRE, which is a general academic preparedness exam. The GMAT is specifically a business school preparedness exam. Two of the three GMAT Focus sections assess quantitative reasoning. If you are good with numbers and quantitative reasoning, you could think about taking the GMAT. Please note that, unless it was clearly stated in the admission requirements, you cannot interchange the GMAT with the GRE; you must submit scores for the exam required by the graduate program.

Importantly, the GMAT has recently undergone significant changes. The new version, called the GMAT Focus, is shorter and contains three, rather than four, sections. The old version will likely be available until early 2024, and then everyone will have to take the new GMAT Focus. According to the test providers, the new GMAT Focus was designed to assess students' ability to analyze data and make good business decisions by interpreting tables, charts, and graphs.

Table 4.

The structure comparison (Sources www.mba.com)

Feature	GMAT Focus (New)	GMAT (Old)
Structure	3 Sections 1. Quantitative Reasoning 2. Verbal Reasoning 3. Data Insight	4 Sections 4. Reasoning 5. Verbal Reasoning 6. Integrated Reasoning 7. Analytical Writing Assessment
Duration	2 hrs 15 min (45 min each)	3 hrs 7 min
Number of questions	64	80
Score scale	205 – 805	200 – 800

131

Let's discuss the content and structure of the GMAT.

Quantitative Reasoning (21 questions, 45 minutes)

The quantitative reasoning section tests numerical literacy, mathematical ability, and problem-solving skills. The questions come from basic mathematics, such as arithmetic and algebra. Test takers are given 21 questions to solve in 45 minutes, which averages to roughly 2.1 minutes per question. This is another difference between the GMAT and the GRE: on the GRE, test takers are given only about 1.6 minutes per question. Each section of the GRE and the GMAT has different average times per question, but, in general, the GMAT provides more time per question than the GRE.

Verbal Reasoning (23 questions, 45 minutes)

Verbal reasoning assesses candidates' reading comprehension and critical reasoning. Reading comprehension involves test takers' ability to understand words and statements. Critical reasoning involves the candidates' ability to draw inferences from written content and to assess arguments. Test takers should have the ability to understand the main idea, supporting idea, inferences, applications, logical structure, and style of a statement. Reading comprehension passages are 350 words or less, followed by a set of questions. Critical reasoning questions come with a short passage (fewer than 100 words) and are followed by a question. According to the GMAT, you do not need to know about the statement's subject to answer the questions correctly.

Data Insight (20 questions, 45 minutes)

This new addition to the GMAT Focus assesses candidates' ability of interpret data in multiple formats, such as reading and understanding tables and graphs. This part was designed to make the test more relevant to today's business world where business leaders have to carefully analyze trends, graphs, charts, and diagrams to understand hidden information. GMAT test takers have to understand and analyze the data provided and make decisions accordingly. This part of the GMAT Focus includes different types of questions, including data sufficiency, graphical interpretation, multi-source reasoning, table and chart analysis, graphics interpretation, and two-part analysis.

The Exam

The GMAT can be take in two ways. If you take the test online, it costs $300. If you take the test at a testing center, it costs $275 (in the United States and Canada). You can pay for the test using a debit or credit card. To register, visit the official GMAT site (www.mba.com). You will need to provide an acceptable ID, which varies country to country, at the time of the exam. For US citizens and residents, valid international travel passports, green cards (permanent resident cards), government-issued driver's licenses, government-issued national/state/province identity cards, and military ID cards are all accepted. In most other countries, GMAT accepts valid international travel passports. However, check your country specific ID requirements before attending the exam.

LSAT (Law School Admission Test)

As indicated by the name, the "Law School Admission Test," or LSAT, is the standardized test for applying to law school. The LSAT is administered by the Law School Admission Council (LSAC), which is a not-for-profit organization. All LSAT related information can be found on the LSAC website (www.lsac.org). I surveyed multiple top law schools in the US and found that many accept both the LSAT and the GRE, including Stanford and Yale law schools.

However, standardized test requirements vary from law school to law school. For example, some law schools request students' entire LSAT or GRE test taking history for admission consideration. That means that if you have taken LSAT exam twice, a university might request your results from both tests. During the pandemic, the Law School Admission Council introduced a remotely proctored online version of the exam called LSAT-Flex, but now it has reverted back to its original LSAT form. For the 2023-2024 testing year, the LSAT fee is $222. Canadian and US citizens and nationals, including DACA grantees who are experiencing financial hardship, may be eligible to apply to a fee waiver program. For more information, go to www.lsac.org, select the LSAT tab, and navigate to the LSAT fee waiver page. Since 2023, LSAC has allowed test takers to choose whether to take the test at home (proctored by a live but remote proctor) or take the exam in person at a digital testing center administered by a third party called Prometric.

The Components Of The Exam

The LSAT is composed of four 35-minute test sections (three section are scored and one unscored). The three scored sections include reading comprehension, analytical reasoning, and logical reasoning. The fourth, unscored variable section allows test administers to validate new test questions for future use. There is a 10-minute break in between the second and third sections, and the whole test takes approximately 3 hours.

Reading Comprehension

This section evaluates the test takers' ability to understand lengthy and complex materials which are very common in law school. The provided text are argumentative, dense, and could be from an unfamiliar subject. Each of the four reading passages is followed by 5-8 questions. These passages are from a wide variety of subjects, ranging from the humanities and social sciences to physical sciences and areas related to the law. The passages are densely written with advanced vocabulary, so test takers should carefully read each passage to accurately understand the web of relationships in the text.

Analytical Reasoning

This section of LSAT is designed to assess test takers' ability to understand facts, rules, and protocols. This section usually comes with single passages followed by a set of questions. The questions and passages are usually not related to law directly, but provide specific details with solid arguments and rules, which still could be relevant to law. Questions that require test takers to reason with conditional statements, make inferences using facts, and recognize logical statements are common in this section. Test takers answer these questions using their knowledge, argumentation skills, and reasoning ability—which are crucial for law school students.

Logical Reasoning

This section assesses a key component of legal analysis: argumentation and analyzing arguments. This section evaluates the test takers' critical reasoning skills, since law students have to analyze, evaluate, construct, and refute arguments. Usually, the passages in this section are not law-related documents. Rather, they are mostly copied from ordinary sources, such as newspapers, magazines, scholarly publications, advertisements, and informal sources. These short passages are followed by one or two questions. Even though the texts are taken from informal sources, the questions are designed to evaluate the test takers' critical thinking and legal reasoning abilities.

MCAT (Medical College Admission Test)

MCAT stands for "Medical College Admission Test," and it is the exam used for applying to medical schools in the United States. The MCAT is also recognized by many other universities across the globe. In addition to medical school admission, the MCAT is an important standardized test for many other health profession-related graduate program. It is a multiple choice standardized test. This exam tests the test takers' problem-solving skills, critical thinking abilities, and their knowledge of natural, behavioral, and social science concepts and principles that are considered prerequisite of medicine. The exam is computer-based and divided into four sections.

Table 5.

MCAT exam structure (Sources: www.aamc.org)

The component	The arrangement	Total questions	Duration
Chemical and Physical Foundations of Biological Systems (Chem/Phys)	• 10 passage-based sets of questions o 4-6 *questions per set* • 15 independent questions	59 questions	95 minutes

Biological and Biochemical Foundations of Living Systems (Bio/Biochem)	• 10 passage-based sets of questions ○ 4-6 questions per set • 15 independent questions	59 questions	95 minutes
Psychological, Social, and Biological Foundations of Behavior (Psych/Soc)	• 10 passage-based sets of questions ○ 4-6 questions per set • 15 independent questions	59 questions	95 minutes
Critical Analysis and Reasoning Skills	• 9 passages ○ 5-7 questions per passage	53 questions	90 minutes

The sections on natural and social sciences are structured around 10 fundamental concepts, referred to as "big ideas," within these fields. Test content is derived from year-long introductory courses encompassing chemistry, physics, biology, biochemistry, psychology, and sociology, as well as organic chemistry. Within these sections, multiple-choice questions prompt test takers to integrate their scientific knowledge across various disciplines along with their scientific inquiry and reasoning abilities. The Critical Analysis and Reasoning Skills section evaluates test takers' capacity to comprehend and analyze information presented in passages from a diverse array of disciplines within the social sciences and humanities. This segment does not demand any specific content knowledge. The MCAT exam measures how the test takers utilize what they know rather than the amount of information they know.

The Exam

With the small breaks, the exam takers might spend around 7 hours and 30 minutes to complete the entire MCAT exam and it has four sections. Americans are allowed to use state driver's license, passport, or green card as identification before the exam. Canadians have different requirements. You need to confirm your country-specific ID requirements. At the time this book was written, the MCAT exam registration fee was $335 for test takers inside US and Canada. Those applying from outside the US and Canada have to pay an additional international fee. However, many economically disadvantaged individuals and under represented minorities in medicine are allowed to appeal to a fee assistance program for registration. For eligibility requirements, visit the MCAT website (www.aamc.org). Let's discuss the content and structure of the MCAT exam.

Biological and Biochemical Foundations of Living Systems

The section on the biological and biochemical foundations of living systems requires test takers to apply their understanding of biological and biochemical principles along with their analytical and reasoning abilities to solve problems. This segment evaluates functions specific to living organisms, including growth, reproduction, homeostasis, metabolism, sensing and responding to changes, and adaptation. Additionally, it assesses test takers' comprehension of how cells and organ systems act together to carry out the functions, and it prompts test takers to analyze these processes across different levels of biological organization within living systems.

Discipline:

- First-semester biochemistry, 25%

- Introductory biology, 65%

- General chemistry, 5%

- Organic chemistry, 5%

Psychological, Social, and Biological Foundations of Behavior Section

This section assesses test takers' ability to solve problems using their knowledge of scientific fundamentals and scientific inquiry. It evaluates test takers' comprehension of how psychological, social, and biological elements influence individuals' behavior, perceptions, interpersonal dynamics. It addresses correlations between cultural influences, social hierarchy, and well-being. This section emphasizes essential concepts that future doctors must grasp to effectively serve diverse populations and comprehend the impact of behavior on health. Moreover, it highlights the necessity for future medical professionals to be prepared to address the social aspects of medicine.

Discipline:

- Introductory psychology, 65% (subject to +/- 5% change)

- Introductory sociology, 30%

- Introductory biology, 5%

Chemical and Physical Foundations of Biological Systems Section

This segment prompts test takers to use their chemistry and physics fundamentals with their reasoning skills. It evaluates test takers' comprehension of mechanical, physical, and biochemical functions of the human body. Additionally, it assesses their ability to explain how the chemical and physical mechanisms operate in living organisms.

Discipline:

- Introductory biochemistry, 25%

- Introductory biology, 5%

- General chemistry, 30%

- Organic chemistry, 15%

- Introductory physics, 25%

If you plan to apply to medical school, you have no other choice than to take the MCAT. The MCAT is a highly specified standardized test designed for medical education, including both MD programs and other medicine-related graduate programs. If you want to attend medical school, it is advisable to begin planning your career during your undergraduate studies, because medical schools usually request multiple prerequisites. Read these requirements on your dream medical school's MD admission requirements page. These requirements vary from one medical school to another, so plan your medical school journey today without a delay.

CHAPTER 10

VIRTUAL INTERVIEW

For a grad school applicant, a virtual interview invitation means that you have been fast-tracked to admission. Unless you make a big mistake during the interview, you will receive an admission letter. Think about it from the grad school's point of view: the selection committee is mostly comprised of busy faculty. They do not want to spend half an hour to one hour of their valuable time with one candidate if that candidate is not qualified enough for the program. So, if you have been invited to interview, they have a serious interest in you.

Even though this chapter is titled "Virtual Interview," the content refers to phone interviews as well. Since the pandemic, grad schools often use virtual interviews as a part of their admission process. Plan to attend a few minutes early in case there are technical issues. If the interview panel is not ready, they will likely put you in a virtual waiting room. If you are admitted to the interview ahead of time, chat with those on the call about casual topics, like the weather, the location, or the university.

Dress Nicely

The word "nice" is subjective; the goal is to be professional and confident in what you wear for a virtual interview. Based on my observation of the natural sciences fields (chemistry, biology, physics, mathematics, etc.), a strict dress code is not highly enforced, but that does not mean you should attend a virtual interview in your pajamas. Business casual attire is appropriate. Overdressing is not frowned upon but underdressing is. Application review panels at professional schools, like business schools, law schools, and medical schools, expect interviewees to dress formally. In some interviews, the required attire is mentioned in the invitation.

As you choose your clothes, consider comfort. Assume you bought the nicest suit for $700 in an effort to impress the panel. But your unfamiliar formal clothing and overly tight tie made you exceptionally nervous and uncomfortable, and as a result you stumbled through the interview. In that case, overdressing sabotaged the interview. Wearing expensive clothing and too much makeup is not recommended. Aim to look pleasant and neat.

Another important note about dressing for virtual interviews is to always wear an appropriate top AND bottom. Some people think they can get away with wearing business casual on top and pajama pants on the bottom, but this is a mistake. What if you have to stand up to get a book or a document, and the interviewers see your shorts? What if the interviewers accidently see your pajama pants when you move? That would be unprofessional. So, wear a complete business casual outfit. There is one caveat to this advice—shoes are not important. The interviewers will not check your shoe brand.

Be Yourself

Usually interview panels are friendly in a formal way, so be yourself and be confident. The panel already knows your qualifications. They might already have your application on their screens. They need to know it is truly you that who accomplished all the achievements listed. They are wondering, did you do really this research and training?

Let me tell you a story about a time when an institution where I was working needed to recruit a batch of students for our undergraduate program. It was a specialized program, so we decided to include an interview in our selection process. Most of the shortlisted applicants were recent high school graduates. One shortlisted applicant who had decent qualifications acted very unusually during his interview. The interview panel asked very basic questions, such as, What are your expectations? Why did you choose this program? The applicant said he had no idea for most of the questions and acted confused. The interview panel was very disappointed and reviewed the applicant's application again. It appeared that his application was fully prepared by his parents. We had enough openings in our program that he could have been admitted, but the interview panel disqualified this applicant. The interview panel needs to know that you match the person portrayed in your application materials.

Do Your Homework (Search)

It is very important to find out who is going to interview you. Usually, your interview invitation will mention the names of the individuals on the panel, or your interview invitation may be cc'd to the panel members. If there is no indication of the panel members, request details from your point of contact, such as the program coordinator or the department secretary (or the office manager).

After you receive the details, start your search. Find out the panel members' affiliations, department, ongoing research, research interests, grants received, classes they teach, education, and institutes where they studied. Read their information in the university directory. This information will prepare you to answer their questions. Find their profile on platforms such as LinkedIn. Investigate whether you have any mutual contacts with the interview panel individuals.

One time I did my homework before an interview, and during the interview one individual on the panel asked me, "So tell me, what research do you do, qualitative or quantitative?" It was on the tip of my tongue to say, "I did qualitative research for my dissertation." But I backed off and said, "I have experience in both qualitative and quantitative research. My master's was in chemistry, and I did a lot of quantitative studies in chemistry." I did not lie, but I adapted my answer according to the person who asked the question. She was a professor in physics, and her background was in astronomy and statistics, so I think it is unlikely that she would have be pleased if I had said, "Just qualitative."

There are so many times I benefited from reading interviewers' profiles. Even if you do not get an offer, these are the big names of the field you are going to enter. Reading about the professional life of an expert in the field will help shape your professional life.

Location & The Internet

Make sure to find an ideal place for the virtual interview that is quiet and not distracting. This is very important if you are having a phone interview. The other most important thing is to ensure uninterrupted internet connection. Once, a university to which I was accepted conducted a virtual interview to test my teaching abilities, since they had only a few highly-competitive teaching assistant positions. I prepared my lesson very well using a PowerPoint, and I designed a teaching demonstration with a few household materials. I conducted my teaching demonstration well but experienced internet connection issues. I barely heard the questions they asked, and they had difficulty viewing my demonstration. After the interview, one interview panel member told me that even though my teaching demonstration was very interesting, they had a hard time grasping what I did because of the poor internet connection. As a result, they decided to offer the TA position to someone else.

You can test the internet at your current location using google internet speed check (https://fiber.google.com/ speedtest/) or with any of several other free internet speed check websites. For example, Zoom's official minimum requirement for an HD video interview is 1.5 Mbps. In practice, however, at least 10 Mbps of uninterrupted speed is required to conduct a seamless Zoom session. Your internet service provider may offer packages with speeds of up to 300 Mbps, 500 Mbps, and 1 Gbps. However, the actual internet speed at any given time could be much slower than what's advertised for various reasons. If you're experiencing a poor internet connection at home just before the interview, try disconnecting other internet streaming devices. If you want to try a different place, a private study room in a library with high-speed internet is recommended.

Equipment Arrangements

Always test your video call platform before an interview. Most virtual interviews occur over Zoom, Skype, or Microsoft Teams. These three applications have different appearances and interfaces. Since each one operates differently, try to familiarize yourself with the platform before the video call.

During my doctoral studies, I always used Zoom. I had a few very nice backgrounds and knew the scope of the video in my small room. I lived in a one-bedroom apartment at that time, so one room served as my study room and my bedroom. I cleared the area that the zoom display covered to make my video calls look professional. One time, I was invited for a virtual job interview via Microsoft Teams. I expected the video to cover the same area of the room as a Zoom call, but I was wrong. The preview window revealed that the clutter in the corner of my room and my messy bed were within the viewing area. Blurring did not help, and I did not know how to add a background at that time in Microsoft Teams. When I was admitted to the meeting, the audio came through the smart speaker in my living room rather than my computer. I quickly apologized and fixed the speaker issues, but the entire drama took me 10 minutes to resolve. The situation was extremely stressful. That's why I recommend arranging a test run of the interview platform before the interview. See how you look on the video. Check how the speakers, webcam, and other instruments work prior to the interview, and you may avoid significant stress and unprofessionalism.

Tricky Questions

On rare occasions, you will be provided with interview questions prior to the interview. If you are given the questions, do not draft answers and read them during the interview. That would be awkward and noticeable. In most cases, interview panels do not share their list of questions so they have flexibility during the interview. Usually, these interviews contain a mixture of simple questions that are easy to answer and a few tricky questions. Try to see each question as an opportunity to add value to your profile. Let's say your first question is, "Tell us about yourself." Rather than just stating your name, university, and program of study, elaborate. Answer, "I am Trent. I recently graduated from the University of Pennsylvania with a degree in chemistry and a minor in mathematics with a 3.8 GPA. My research was in microwave spectroscopy."

Always make your answers relevant to the current position. Imagine you were applying to the school that has the best microwave spectrometer in the country and that the spectroscopy professor was in the interview panel. You would want to elaborate a bit on what did you do in your spectroscopy research.

The panel may want to know why you applied to this university. You could say the importance of the institution attracted you. You could mention motivating factors, such as aligned research interests, the quality and the reputation of the program, research panel, etc. If your siblings or family member graduated, studied, or worked at this university, you could mention that. If you live in Indianapolis, Indiana and applied to Purdue University, you could mention the draw of close proximity. But if you were admitted to an Ivy League school, using location proximity may not be considered an advantage. The panel may ask what other universities you have applied to and received admission from. This is a tricky question, and you do not need to provide all the information requested. While sharing a few places that you applied to and offers you received, you could highlight your desire to attend this university for a few specific reasons (provide the reasons).

Strengths & Weaknesses

You may receive a tricky question about your strengths and weaknesses. Be prepared to mention a few strengths that are very relevant to your studies. Say that you are always curious to learn, that you are a fast learner, and that you excel at teamwork.

Responding to questions about your weaknesses can be more difficult. Do not mention any weakness that would badly affect your resume. Mention a weakness that is irrelevant or passively benefits your academics. Say that you have a bad habit of working around the clock until you complete your work. The panel would love that weakness. Perfectionism is another acceptable weakness, as are being impatient for more data, overthinking, and trying to handle too much. These are just a few examples. Remember: always be honest. These are a few common weaknesses that most of us experience during our academic journey. If you feel you have any of these weaknesses, share them to avoid undermining the panel's confidence in you.

Another tricky question I was once asked by a panel was to "explain a challenge that you think you handled successfully." Do not share anything personal, such as relationship challenges. These people are still strangers to you. Try to provide an example of an academic or professional challenge that you tackled. You may be wondering, "Should I explain how I changed my research supervisor during my senior year?" You could, but this might negatively affect your image, and the panel may worry that history will repeat itself. Think of something to share to elevate your professional and academic image.

Gratitude

Show your enthusiasm to be accepted to the particular program. Ask what will happen next, and the panel may provide relevant details. Be professional, genuine, and honest during the interview. After you complete your interview, you may send an e-mail thanking the individual who participated in the interview panel. Send them your gratitude quickly— they will make your admission decision soon.

CHAPTER 11

CAMPUS VISIT

You will be invited to visit campus after you have been accepted to a graduate program. If you have not received an acceptance letter but still receive a campus visit invitation, that is a good sign that you will be selected or that you are at least on the waitlist. Campus visits are a great way to learn more about campuses, grad schools, and grad programs and determine how well you may fit in each program. If you receive an invitation for a grad school visit, accept it without hesitation. You have nothing to lose. Visiting multiple campuses can help you to compare different programs and find the best program for you.

Funding For Campus Visits

In STEM fields, most applicants to graduate programs (especially doctoral programs) receive fully paid campus visits. Their transportation (air tickets, shuttle tickets, or mileage), lodging, and food are paid for by the university. Think of it like a small vacation where you do not have to pay for anything. Some schools and programs fund their prospective grad students' campus visits. Some schools may arrange accommodation during the stay but leave transportation arrangements to the incoming students. Some programs announce just an open day for interested grad school applicants to attend. In the case of such open invitations, the school does not pay for anything. This open day concept is more common among master's level programs. Since the pandemic, more grad school programs conduct their grad school visits virtually.

Plan Your Visit

If you really want to attend a particular university or graduate program, you might choose that graduate program whether or not you visit the campus. However, most prospective students apply to multiple programs and receive several offers. If you are in this situation, campus visits can provide clarity and help you decide which offer to accept. Plan your campus visit in advance. Campus visits are enjoyable; they are organized for you and tailored for your graduate education needs. You will receive a campus visit agenda, which will include an opportunity to meet the program faculty, graduate coordinator, current graduate students, administrative staff, and maybe undergraduate students. There will be plenty of time to meet faculty and graduate students over lunch or coffee. While you can enjoy the program's hospitality, you also need to plan your own agenda to gain the maximize your visit. Plan to meet the most important personnel and visit the important resources that you would think will be most vital for your graduate studies.

The invitation should provide most of the information you need about your visit, but you should plan your stay effectively. Do not forget to meet faculty (at least two or three) whom you would like to work with. E-mail them in advance, explaining your interest and your willingness to meet them. They will respond more readily at this point since you have received the offer letter. If they do not respond, you can follow up.

Faculty will take different approaches to meeting with you. Some may ask you to meet them in their office for a formal conversation. Some of them may invite you to their lab and offer you a lab visit. Some of them may invite you to the cafeteria for a coffee, others will only engage in brief introductions, and others simply won't be willing or able to meet because they are busy.

Dress Code

Dress nicely and professionally. Your invitation may mention a dress code, or you can ask your point of contact about the dress code. Usually in academia, formal appearance is not as important as at a professional school, but business casual is always safe. For men, a buttoned shirt, dress pants, dress shoes, and an optional tie is great. I personally prefer a sweater. A coat is optional. For women, a fitted blouse, dress slack, toe shoes (with moderate to low heel), and an optional jacket is great. Do not wear too much jewelry or makeup and avoid very high heels.

Again, even though this is generic advice for a dress code, do not wear anything beyond your comfort zone. If you are a girl with luminous green hair, you do not need to bleach it the day before the campus visit. If you are a man who usually wears earrings, wear them during your campus visit. If you are a trans girl, wear the appropriate clothing to suit your representation. I believe higher education has greater tolerance of different and unique identities than the rest of society. Observe how faculty and your future colleagues respond to you. If you feel like you don't belong or aren't welcome, let that inform your decision. You deserve respect. Also, always be respectful of your campus hosts.

Explore The Ambiance

Observe the department, how the program runs, and how colleagues interact with each other. Take in the classrooms, laboratories, libraries, cafeterias, and other facilities. Probe graduate student welfare, faculty/student interactions, grad student/undergraduate student interactions, and the general attitude of nonacademic and administrative staff towards grad students. Remember, during your campus visit the department or the program of study will present the best image of themselves, but programs are not always as good as they appear. Getting a master's or a PhD is not easy, so choosing a program that is a good fit is critical. During your campus visits, try to find the answers to your most critical questions.

Make Contacts

You will likely encounter friendly graduate students during your campus visits who may offer to give you a tour around the department. Accept such offers gratefully. These offers not only mean a chance to see the campus, but also an opportunity to hear graduate students' thoughts on their campus and program. This is not a Q&A session, so try not to make it awkward. Just have a friendly conversation and listen to the details that they provide related to campus life and the graduate program.

Think of such interactions as an opportunity to expand your network. Even if you do not ultimately attend this school, you will likely see these students and faculty again at conferences, job talks, and maybe even your future workplaces. So, try to interact with them nicely. During my campus visits, I met many awesome people (faculty, grad students, and undergrad students), and I still continue my professional connections with them today.

Ask And Find

During the campus visit you will mostly interact with the people of your program of study. Make sure to talk with faculty, graduate students, and administrative staff. Take a moment to have a polite, friendly, and professional conversation with as many as possible to learn about the program. Below are a few questions to help you get started, but you can also prepare more questions to suit your situation.

- How many doctoral/master's students have graduated from this program with a job?

- Is the graduate stipend enough to live on?

- How many students have dropped out from the program in last few years?

- How many years does a doctoral/master's student usually take to complete the program?

- How many years of funding are available?

- How good are student health and welfare benefits?

- How safe is the campus and the area surrounding the campus?

- What do you like most about the program?

- What do you least like about the program?

Before your visit, make a list of questions you want to ask during your campus visits. I remind you again, your conversations with students and faculty are not Q&A sessions. Just be prepared to ask these questions whenever you find the right person and an appropriate time. For example, faculty usually do not know about the student welfare package. You need to reach out a senior graduate student to ask questions about that. Likewise, the number of years funding is available for grad students is a question to ask the graduate program coordinator.

Choosing the #1 Program

I understand that you are determined to attend the best-ranked and most prestigious university in your field. That is great. This entire book is written as a guide

168

to getting accepted to your dream grad school. However, I need to add a little sidenote as well. During these last couple of years, I have observed several doctoral students experience unfortunate situations. I can give you one example. Several of my colleagues were drawn to a prestigious university for their graduate studies. Many of my colleagues were fortunate (or unfortunate) enough to admit to that university. After a few years of struggle, many of them changed their program of study, and some of them even dropped out without getting a master's degree.

It is common for a program to have a couple students over the years who change their program of study or drop out from the program. But if this happens often, it is a big red flag. If students of one particular supervisor often fail their qualifying exams or are unable to fulfill their portfolio, you should be cautious on choosing that supervisor as your supervisor. This kind of information is hidden unless you specifically ask. You have enough time to mingle with grad students. Ask them questions, be polite, and they will help you. The department cannot do anything against you for asking such questions, because you have already received an acceptance letter. While you are chasing the top-ranked university, consider how this program fits you with your future in mind.

More Things To Consider

You will meet many graduate students during your visit. Usually, one or two graduate students are assigned to assist prospective students during campus visits. They may pick you up from the airport or shuttle station and drive you to your accommodation, and they will be your guides on campus. Ideally, the volunteer will be a part of the program you are interested in, allowing you to ask specific questions. It is very important to understand the working environment and the ambience in the department, since these may affect your decision. One of my colleagues told me that the moment she saw the amount of analytical chemistry equipment lined up in the labs, she decided to accept that university's offer. When I was attending campus visits, I was mostly fascinated by the friendliness of the graduate cohort and the close connection they maintained between the faculty and graduate students. Another colleague of mine was really motivated to attend a particular graduate school because of the gigantic gymnasium located next to his department, and he is still excelling in that academic program.

Be Yourself

During the entire stay, make sure to be yourself. Do not try to act like a nerdy young Sheldon Cooper to please anybody. The faculty and graduate students are eager to get to know you better. You being yourself helps you to understand whether would you fit in this place (or not). I have discussed extensively in this book how to be yourself. Dress professionally but do not try to impersonate anyone. Act professionally but do not try to impersonate Albert Einstein or some other scholar. You are just a grad applicant who received an admission offer; there is no shame in not knowing things at this point. Also, being yourself will help you to understand things faster. Be polite and friendly. Ask questions and be curious. Also don't miss the fun part. Enjoy the hospitality and make connections.

Ask About Housing

If you have not yet found an apartment or housing, ask the graduate students about housing. They can give you the best information about the current student housing and renting situation in town. They can tell you about the ideal neighborhoods and rental properties that grad students should choose and which places to avoid. Get this valuable information. Your point of contact and the administrative staff, but usually not faculty, can also be good resources for housing information. If you do not have enough time to visit a few housing locations, get the details of the rental places to contact them later.

After The Campus Visit

Enjoy your stay. When you have returned, do not forget to send thank you letters or an e-mail to each person who helped you and anybody else you think you should thank. Think about the entire stay and reflect on how you feel. You may still have some details to clarify, but you have gotten many contacts. Use those contacts to ask for more details. Sometimes it is hard to pick one school out of many if you have received multiple admissions. I recommend waiting for a while after your campus visit until the excitement is gone to reconsider the offer. Technically you could wait until the deadline to accept or drop the offer, but if you have already decided, do not wait to inform the schools. When you drop an offer, someone like you on the waitlist may receive the opportunity to admit to that grad program.

CHAPTER 12

ONLINE VS RESIDENTIAL DEGREES

There are online master's programs in some fields, but the American university system prefers to keep their doctoral students in-person to do research. Before the pandemic hit, it was rare to find online doctoral programs in the United States. Today, as a result of the pandemic, there are more part-time and distance learning opportunities available. Yet it is still standard for master's and doctoral programs in the natural sciences, such as chemistry, physics, and biology, to be fulltime in-person. To earn a PhD in those fields you have to spend years doing research. Additionally, after completing a PhD, you will be a researcher, and anyone interested in hiring you will be concerned about your ability to conduct research independently, not about the courses you completed. If a university in the United States advertises a remote doctoral program in the natural sciences, examine the details carefully and think twice before pursuing it.

EdD and other doctorates in specific fields are different. Even the Harvard graduate school of education conducts EdD programs online. In the humanities, social sciences, education, business, and information technology fields there are a considerable amount of online master's programs are available. Some of these online programs are delivered by well-reputed universities, while others are overly priced, substandard programs. This chapter is written to help you spot good graduate programs (online or residential), avoid substandard programs, and enroll in your ideal graduate program. Let's talk about the pros and cons of pursuing an online graduate program versus an in-person graduate program.

Accessibility and Flexibility

Accessibility and flexibility can be considered the biggest advantages of online graduate programs. My masters and PhD both were in-person programs, so I had to relocate to pursue my studies. For some of you, that might be a deal breaker. When relocation is not possible, pursuing a graduate degree online is advisable.

Sometimes courses in online programs are conducted asynchronously, allowing students to watch pre-recorded videos of lecture instead of attending a class virtually at a specific time each week. Most of these courses replace exams with projects and assignments, eliminating the challenge of attending exams. As there is no limit on students, or geographical location, a diverse group of students from across the country, and maybe even around the world, may participate in the program.

On Your Own Pace

Not all grad students approach academics the same way. Some prefer a slower pace or need to watch lectures multiple times to grasp the material, so online, asynchronous programs are a good fit for these students. Some online graduate programs are designed with rolling assignment deadlines so that whenever students complete their coursework, they can submit it. Such programs do not have hard semester lines. When the students finish the course, they can submit it, no matter how long it takes. Some students can take more classes and finish their degree sooner, while students who prefer a slower pace can take longer. In-person graduate courses do not offer such flexibility.

Cost and Time

If you study online, you do not have to worry about the costs of relocation, and rent, that are involved in moving. Online programs are now provided at a cheaper cost (per credit hour) than residential programs. Online programs typically do not have different in-state and out-of-state rates. With online programs, you do not have a daily commute to campus, saving you time and money. The time you have in between classes can be utilized for something useful at your home or work place. However, residential students are typically prioritized for teaching assistantships and other funding opportunities. Usually, doctoral programs consist of a minimum of 90 credits (for most PhDs) to complete, so if you attend a virtual program, you will have to pay a lot of money out of pocket or take out significant student loans.

G Credits

I am mentioning this problem because, at the time this book was written, one private for-profit university is in a lawsuit on the G credit issue. Usually after doctoral students complete their required coursework, they have to conduct additional research. This research might take a year, two years, or even more to complete. Throughout these years, doctoral candidates must maintain their active student status by taking research credits. Usually those are called G credits. As those credits do not have any coursework requirements, G credits are available at a cheaper price. (When I was doctoral student, one G credit costs $100, while one doctoral credit cost $1350 at an out-of-state student rate.) If a doctoral student takes longer to complete their research, upstanding universities will offer them the lower-priced G credits to maintain their active student status. However, some private for-profit universities do not offer such assistance, which could badly damage your financial situation.

Interaction

Student and teacher interaction is very important for graduate students. Even during the pandemic when the schools were fully online, I tried to meet with my teachers virtually during their office hours to discuss important topics. Some students need this interaction. Large and reputable American universities are designed for students to learn from everything on campus from the library, to peers, seminars, and trainings. That might be the reason these institutions are called universities. Online and part-time learners might miss some of these learning opportunities.

During my master's, we had biweekly mandatory seminars. All the participants were served pizza as we heard from a field expert about their research and had the opportunity to ask questions and engage in discussion. During my doctoral studies, the school conducted a program called the Brown Bag series. Biweekly the grad school brought a resource person to talk about career development, job applications, and other opportunities. I learned a lot from the talks, and I enjoyed the provided lunch food. Online students might miss such valuable opportunities.

Networking

Those with higher level graduate qualifications, such as PhDs and other doctorate degrees, need a good network to become established in their field. Graduate students attending residential programs may have more opportunities than those enrolled in online programs to interact with professionals, mentors, industry leaders and peers (inside and outside of their school). During your graduate program, when you attend conferences, seminars, webinars, and field visits, your supervisor or the graduate coordinator will likely introduce you to her or his colleagues. In each field study, the academia and the faculty professionals are close knit and know each other professionally and perhaps even personally. Such networking is important when you are applying for jobs.

In-person grad level programs offer plenty of networking opportunities. I know there are good EdD and other online doctoral degrees in which the program coordinators motivate their students to attend conferences, apply for grants, and guide them to publish their research. If such support mechanisms are absent in an online program (specifically in a doctoral program), it might not be considered a good doctoral program. At the master's level, conducting research and publishing are not given the highest priority. However, apart from academics, there must be a good professional development (PD) mechanism at the master's level.

Reputation

Critically, PhD, EdD, MS, and MA, are not acronyms for standards; they are acronyms for graduate level education qualifications. The standard or quality of these educational qualifications is often connected to the institution where the degree was earned. To illustrate this, imaging that two people are in a conversation, and one mentions that she has recently completed her PhD. The second person's likely responses is, "Congratulations! Where did you graduate from?" That is a standard follow-up question because different educational institutions have different educational standards.

Prestigious universities hold their students to higher standards. I have had experience being a student at three graduate educational institutes in the United States. Two of them are R-1 level large research universities, and one is a regional university. They each have different educational standards. Also, in education, the institution from which you graduate is kind of like a brand. If you attend a top-ranking university, the prestige of that university elevates your professional image.

High-ranking research universities, like R1 universities including Ivy League universities, maintain robust graduate programs, and their strong research activities benefit their doctoral students. Degrees from such institutions are held in high esteem across academia and professional sectors. The Carnegie Classification of Institutions of Higher Education categorizes high-level research universities. You can find the up-to-date list of R1 level Doctoral Universities: Very High Research Activity on the Carnegie Classification website (https://

carnegieclassifications.acenet.edu/institutions/> Filter: Basics: Doctoral Universities > Very high research activities). In contrast, there are commercial for-profit universities (which sometimes advertise themselves as non-profit) which often invest less in their students. While such universities may offer good undergraduate programs, and maybe even decent master's programs, I am not fully confident that they can deliver high-quality doctoral programs. You may think your desired doctorate could be bought from such a university, but the reality is that such programs give you nothing but debt. People in academia and many in the corporate sector in your field know which institutions have rigorous programs and which have programs of little value, so a doctoral degree from such substandard institutions may be worth very little to you despite the steep price. I urge you to find an accredited university from which to earn your degree.

Admission Requirements

At most accredited and well-reputed universities, the admission requirements are considerably higher than at other universities. If you are applying to a doctoral program, they expect you to have a certain amount of graduate level courses, a good undergraduate GPA, strong recommendations, solid standardized test scores, and good language proficiency test scores (when applicable). If the program is more competitive, the admission requirements are even higher.

Let's take the Wharton's MBA admission requirements as an example. Wharton is the renowned business school of the University of Pennsylvania and one of the best business schools of the nation. The application process requires two to three essays instead of a general statement of purpose. They have specific requirements for recommendation letters, stating who is eligible to submit a letter and what they should write.

Your goal should be to get accepted to a school and a program with a strong reputation, not a school that has low standards for admission. If your profile is not strong enough yet, strengthen it. We have discussed many ways to build a strong application and be a competitive grad school candidate.

Mentor and Teaching Cohort

Potential mentors are another important factor to consider as you evaluate graduate schools. Your mentor during your graduate studies will have a significant influence on your transition to the job market. You earn a graduate qualification to advance your future career, and having an excellent mentor or a supervisor is an added advantage for your resume.

Top universities do not always house the best professors; sometimes the most renowned professors work at small regional universities. So, it is important to know the teaching and researching faculty at the universities you have applied to before accepting an admission offer. To find this information, read the program's websites. Most reputable universities proudly showcase their teaching cohort, highlighting their educational backgrounds and qualifications. If a graduate program of a university does not provide proper information on their teaching cohort and their qualifications, consider it a red flag. This is not your undergraduate degree; it is crucial to learn from well-qualified professors at the graduate level.

If a university page does not provide enough information about the curriculum, teaching cohort, admission requirements, tuition, and fees of the program, but recruitment officers are rushing your admission, that could also be suspicious. Usually, reputable universities provide all this information on their website. If you are concerned, find the Harvard, Yale, Stanford, or your home state's flagship university's information page for the graduate program you are interested in. Compare that information page with the information page of a doubtful university and identify any concerning differences.

PhD vs EdD

Many people do not know the difference between a PhD and an EdD. While these degrees technically differ, their practical applications overlap significantly. PhD stands for Doctor of Philosophy, while EdD stands for Doctor of Education. There are other doctorate level degrees in other fields as well, such as Doctor of Business Administration (DBA) and Doctor of Human resources (D-HR). However, in all fields of study, there are related PhDs. I received my doctoral degree (a PhD, not an EdD) in Science Education.

Usually, a PhD is considered a research degree that makes the holder qualified to conduct research. PhD holders are also qualified to teach and take positions in academia. In contrast, an EdD has more practical applications. For example, EdD holders are more qualified to be educational administrators. But both of PhDs and EdDs are considered terminal degrees, so those with either degree could be qualified for many job positions and tasks. While PhD students study more theoretical topics, EdD students study more application-oriented topics. For this reason, there are more online EdD programs and other subject specific doctorates than online PhDs.

Choose Wisely

Promoting residential degrees and discouraging online degrees is not the goal of this chapter. Not all online degrees are bad. At the moment, I am taking graduate level classes online from a R1 level university, and I love the program. Neither can we say all residential graduate programs are good. The main goal of this chapter is to provide you with enough information to choose the best program for you, whether online or residential. Choose a graduate program that will benefit your career the most. Choose the best program to elevate your professional and academic level. There are many great graduate programs in the United States that may fit your career and academic requirements. So, use this information and choose wisely.

Reference

- Carnegie classification of institutions of higher education (https://carnegieclassifications.acenet.edu/instituti ons).

CHAPTER 13

HOUSING

Finding housing as a graduate student can be more challenging than finding housing as an undergraduate. Undergraduates tend to have more housing options, and they tend to be less picky when choosing roommates and housing. Graduate students who have had previous experience with roommates may be more cautious. Personally, I have had awesome roommates that made sharing my apartment's common area and kitchen easy. Unfortunately, I have also had negative experiences with bad roommates who even stole my food. You have to be careful when choosing your roommate. There are different housing options available to grad students, and you may choose to live with or without roommates. This chapter offers advice and

191

guidance as you navigate graduate school housing decisions.

Start Early

Don't wait until the last minute to begin your housing search. Large research universities and flagship universities increase their student intake every year, but their housing capacity does not increase proportionately. If you are going to attend a large university in a campus town, this will impact you. So, start as soon as possible. In campus towns, the housing market usually runs according to the campus academic calendar. Try to visit the property before you sign the lease. If you are not able to, reach out to any friends or colleagues who live in the property to ask them about it.

On-Campus Housing And Dorms

One of the most important decisions you have to make when looking for housing is whether you prefer on-campus or off-campus housing. On-campus living is convenient, and it may be relatively cheaper than many outside apartments. Usually, all utilities are included in campus housing, so tenants do not have to pay additional utility fees. If you worry about utility bills, campus housing would be a good place for you.

However, on-campus housing is not a good fit for people who worry about privacy. Campus housing options are often multi-floored buildings on the campus premises. Most of the time the surroundings are busy. On the day of large sporting events, campus housing can feel like home arrest with jammed roads, crowds on the sidewalks, and an overloaded shuttle service. Campus housing often has shared corridors connecting the living spaces of other graduate and undergraduate students. Even if you enjoyed living on campus as an undergraduate, you need to consider whether your expectations and lifestyle have changed. If you feel that you are still the same old undergraduate social butterfly, campus housing could be a good choice for you.

Another concern with campus housing is internet privacy. Campus housing comes with campus Wi-Fi, and most universities have restrictions and guidelines for campus internet usage. If you are really interested in choosing on campus housing, read the internet privacy policy and the lease agreement carefully before you move in.

Graduate Housing

At some universities, graduate housing could be a very good option. However, not all universities have enough graduate housing. Usually, graduate housing comes as an apartment with one or two bedrooms that fit a small family. Utilities are typically included. Some graduate housing is furnished and some is unfurnished. You need to find these details before moving in.

I have visited the on-campus graduate housing of my colleagues. Most of the buildings are old and the units are basic. But for the low rent, it is well worth it. In most cases, graduate housing residents are considered part of the graduate housing community and may be requested to contribute some amount of community work. When graduate housing openings are limited, you might have to be on a wait list for months. At some universities, priority is given to families over single individuals. No matter your situation, arrange your housing as soon as you accept an offer.

Off-Campus Housing

I have observed that graduate students tend to prefer off-campus housing. Off-campus housing could be a little more expensive than on-campus housing, but there are more options and variety. Off-campus housing is owned by private landlords. These rental units are located around campus, but, if you choose to live off-campus, you need to think about the commute and transportation as well. The town where I did my master's did not have any public transportation (very common in small Midwest college towns). I was able to find an off-campus apartment right across from my department. Some of my colleagues moved into off-campus apartments near campus. Later, they realized that there was no public transportation in the town and that the school shuttle did not cover the area where they lived. So they were forced to buy old used cars and old bicycles to commute. Transporting a week's worth of groceries from Walmart on a bicycle was not fun. So, pay attention to transportation if you are planning to live off-campus. Some apartments offer their own shuttle services. That is also convenient. But make sure that you consider all of these things before you sign a lease.

In addition to transportation, you need to think about other arrangements as well. One is the laundry situation. Another is whether you prefer an upstairs or downstairs unit. Many say the ground floor is the best, but I would say both upstairs and downstairs have pros and cons. Ground level units are more convenient, since you do not need to climb stairs to access the apartment. You can do jumping jacks without disturbing anyone. Usually, ground floor units are more insulated — and warmer — than top floor units below the roof. So, ground floor residence can save money on heating. On the other hand, upstairs can be better because you do not have to worry about noise coming from the floor above you. If there is a plumbing issue, upstairs is the safest place, while ground floors could be easily flooded. Consider all these things before you sign a lease.

Neighborhoods

When searching for off-campus housing, consider the location carefully. Look for neighborhoods that are safe by checking crime maps. Properties in safer neighborhoods are relatively more expensive than those in other areas, but it is worth it to pay a little extra for your safety. Talk to current graduate students about the housing situation in the local neighborhood.

Also, you need to think about public transportation and the commute to campus. Take into account factors such as proximity to grocery stores, libraries, and other amenities that are important to you. If you are a medical student or a nursing student, and you need to commute often to your clinical facilities and the hospital, take that into account as well.

Roommates

I could write a whole chapter, if not a book, about roommates. I have had plenty of experience with how a good roommate can make your life comfortable and how a bad roommate can make your life miserable. You likely want a roommate to share the cost of rent. You may want a roommate for company. Either way, you should find a suitable roommate for your lifestyle and needs. It is always better to find a roommate from your university. Finding a roommate from the same program of study is even better. As you are a grad student, it is safest to find a grad student, rather than an undergrad student, as a roommate. Usually grad students have a different, more regular lifestyle than undergraduates. Sometimes universities have portals for internal roommate searches. There are also university-specific roommate-seeking Facebook pages. I recommend looking for roommates in such places rather finding strangers on Craigslist.

If you are looking for a roommate, make sure you write a good description about yourself and clearly explain any deal breakers. For example, I am allergic to cats, so I can never move in with a roommate who has a cat. Assume you are a queer guy and you do not mention your sexual orientation in the post. Imagine how your life would be if you chose a roommate who does not tolerate you. So, make things clear before you move in.

If you think you have found a potential roommate, invite him or her to coffee to find out if you are a good fit. The 20 bucks you spend on Starbucks would not be wasted. Discuss your common interests, bathroom times, kitchen use, common space use, cleaning expectations, noise levels, usual bedtime/quiet time, etc. If two bedrooms are located next to each other, you have to be very considerate about the noise level. If your potential roommate lives far away, you can have a zoom call to discuss these. You need to know these things beforehand, because once you sign the lease with your new roommate, it is hard to change it for another year.

Furnishing Your Apartment

You are a college student. You may have an assistantship or you might not. You might work off campus. Either way, as a graduate student, you will not have money to buy fancy brand new furniture. If the apartment is unfurnished, the first thing to buy is your bed, or else at least the mattress, because good sleep is essential. You can survive without a working table and a chair for a week or two—the library is more than adequate for your study needs. The rest you can buy secondhand at used furniture companies and thrift stores. In most college towns, charity organizations help incoming students settle in. I received a lot of my furniture and plenty of pots and pans from such charitable organizations. There might be a few of such organization in your college town as well.

If you are admitting to a master's level program and moving to the college town from elsewhere, it is recommended to find a furnished apartment, because you will only stay there for two years. Master's programs are designed to be completed in two years and are mostly predictable. If you are enrolling in a doctoral program, you can move into an unfurnished apartment and spend some money on used furniture, because you will live there for a considerable amount of time (probably more than four years). PhDs are not designed to be completed in a particular timeframe. You will finish it when you finish it or when your supervisor says you have completed it. It is unpredictable.

Read The Lease Agreement

Before signing the lease, carefully review the terms and conditions. In most cases you have room to change the conditions before you sign the lease. Once you sign the lease, you do not have the ability to change anything. Reading the lease helps you understand your responsibilities and your rights. A lease is a 10 to 15 pages long, boring document, but it is important to pay attention to move in date, move out date, security deposits, pet policies, parking, utilities policies, laundry, common space uses, backyard and front, etc. Believe me, reading this document will save you money and time.

Documentation

When applying for housing, be prepared to provide documentation, such as proof of income, references, and rental history. When you visit the apartment in person, bring all these documents. Your landlords may also require a credit check or background check as part of the application process. Usually, you are not allowed to move in until your credit check and background check are approved.

When I got my first job offer (while I was in grad school), I toured potential future apartments. While I identified my top choice, my second-best choice apartment complex manager gave me an offer. She said that if I signed the lease the same day, I would get my own brand-new washer and dryer. That was a very good deal. I brought all my documents (an offer letter, pay slips, bank details, etc.), signed the lease, and moved in. I never regretted my decision.

CHAPTER 14

INTERNATIONAL APPLICANTS

The United States has become a popular destination for international graduate students. According to National Science Foundation (NSF) data, more than 40% of all American STEM doctoral students are foreign-born. Yet international students can face unique challenges in the grad school application process. In this chapter, I'll explain a few key aspects of American graduate school programs and their application processes to help international students better prepare.

It's important to note before getting into the details that the graduate school application process is lengthier for international students than for domestic students, because international students have to demonstrate that they meet all the American standards and university requirements. I'd recommend that international applicants start the process earlier than the model application timeline provided in this book.

Degree Requirements

An American undergraduate degree is typically a four-year academic qualification with 120 college credits. Including my home country, most British Commonwealth countries conduct three-year undergraduate programs. If you have completed a three-year degree and plan to apply to a US grad school, it is highly recommended to fill the gap with a one- or two-year master's program as a substitute for the undergraduate credit requirement.

If your home country undergraduate degree qualification is a degree equivalent and needs to be evaluated according to American credit standards, you can evaluate your undergraduate education credentials using World Education Services (www.wes.org). I have evaluated my credentials using World Education Services. Please note that you have to choose American standards when you order documents. This service is popular among Canadian immigrants, but the Canadian evaluation is not accepted for US graduate admission.

Sending Transcripts

Sending transcripts was one challenge I faced as an international student applicant. If you graduate from an American university, you can send your transcripts electronically. Unfortunately, that privilege is not available to most international applicants, who instead have to ask their home institution to send their original transcripts to the grad school on their behalf. Since most US institutions do not accept transcripts sent through email, hard copies of the transcripts must be mailed in a secure way. I had to send transcripts from three different institutes in my home country. Those three institutes each sent the transcripts a different way.

I strongly recommend using a courier service rather than sending your transcripts through regular mail. This ensures that you know when the transcripts are delivered. While your documents are in transit, keep an eye on your grad application portal. If the portal does not indicate that your transcript has been delivered after the courier service indicates that it has been delivered, contact the grad office. DHL, FedEx, and UPS are all international courier services that deliver mail to the United States. These services offer discounts for educational document deliveries and student applicants. Contact your courier service country office for more information.

Master's or PhD

Many international applicants ask whether to apply for a master's or a PhD program. There are pros and cons to both, but my personal recommendation is to apply for a PhD program rather than a master's. If you are intently focused on your career and have enough liquid funds for two years of tuition and living expenses, a master's degree could be feasible. However, in the United States, PhD positions offer a stipend and tuition remission more often than master's degrees. If you decide to work in the United States and plan to apply for green card, a PhD would make you more eligible.

Funding

Funding is very important for international students in the US as they are not allowed to work outside of campus. Unlike other countries, like Australia and New Zealand, the spouse of an international student (who holds an F2 or J2 visa) are also not allowed to work. Therefore, funding availability can be critical. If you are applying for a PhD, you can ask your graduate coordinator about funding. If you are applying for a master's, the situation is a little different. At universities that only have a master's program and not a PhD program for a field, it is possible for a master's student to get funding. However, in an R1 level high research university, it is hard to secure full funding at the master's level.

Language Requirements

Language requirements vary from school to school. Typically, universities determine language requirements by country. Graduate schools often have a list of countries for which they waive the language proficiency test. For example, if you are from England or Australia, the grad school will waive your language proficiency test. I read many grad school admission pages to make a list of countries that are commonly considered English-speaking countries, but the policies varied too much to create a master list. To determine the policies of schools you are applying for, read the international students' admission requirements on the graduate school admission website.

Apart from living in a country that is considered English speaking, you may also be able to avoid taking an English language proficiency test if you completed your undergraduate degree in a country where English is an official language. For example, if you are an Indian student who completed your undergraduate degree at an institute in England, there is a high chance that your IELTS or TOEFL requirement could be waived. Read your grad school English language requirement carefully.

The most common language proficiency test accepted in the United States is the TOEFL (Test of English as a Foreign Language). The IELTS (International English Language Testing System) exam is the most widely accepted test in British Commonwealth countries, and it is also accepted by most American universities. There are two versions of the TOEFL exam: TOEEL iBT and TOEFL Essentials. Academic institutions prefer the TOEFL iBT. Likewise, there are two versions of the IELTS exam: IETLS General (required for immigration purposes) and IELTS Academic. American academic institutions prefer the IELTS Academic test.

IELTS is administered as a written exam with pencil and paper, while the TOEFL exam is computer-based. I prefer writing over typing, so personally I prefer the IELTS. But some exam takers prefer to type, so they prefer the TOEFL exam over the IELTS.

Statement of Purpose

In addition to other information provided in this book, I believe there are two important things international students in particular need to know about their statement of purpose (SOP). First, it is critical not to make any mistakes on your SOP. Compose it, and then comb it carefully several times for spelling and grammar mistakes.

Second, do not be afraid to promote yourself in your SOP. I have read many articles and listened to many international podcasts about how international student applicants tend to be less comfortable with self-promotion than American students. Most international students grow up in societies where self-depreciation and humility are encouraged, while self-promotion is discouraged. This can pose a problem when international students apply at American universities. If you are planning to come to the United States, you need to approach your SOP with an American mindset. Your application reviewers expect to hear your story in your SOP.

Try to promote your story with evidence. Self-promotion is not considered a bad thing in the United States, but you must have enough evidence to support the statements you make. Also, make your self-promotion appealing to the selection committee. Some universities post successful SOPs and SOP templates on their websites. Read those to get an idea of what they expect. Please do not copy samples, though—if you are caught, your application will be rejected.

Educational Agencies

You do not need to request help from private educational agencies to apply to US grad schools.

Australian universities have agents in different countries who act as mediators between applicants and universities. However, this is not practiced in the American university system. You can contact your US university graduate program coordinator directly. These coordinators are usually friendly and happy to help.

Most graduate schools have international grad students that serve as international grad student ambassadors. I was one during my doctoral studies. You can request information from them as well without a mediator. If you are looking for a US government-funded scholarship, you can contact the US Fulbright Commission office in your country (https://us.fulbrightonline.org/, your country office may have a different website). Your country office may also provide consultations on US grad student studies.

Paying for Your Application

There are many costs associated with applying for graduate school, ranging from exam fees to application fees. If you are planning to apply for graduate school in the United States, I recommend applying for a credit card that allows international transactions. You could pay fees associated with the application process with your parents' or someone else's credit card. However, depending on the service provider, your transaction could be denied because the applicant's name and the name on the card are not the same. Unlike domestic transactions, international credit card transactions are usually restricted in most countries.

Having a credit card designated for international transactions can make the process smoother, but you still may run into challenges. I remember when I paid $220 to book my GRE exam, my bank immediately called me to ask whether the payment was made by me or if it was a fraudulent charge.

International Student Offices and the I-20

One area of American universities that international students often struggle with is the international office. All American universities maintain high standards and treat graduate applicants and students with integrity and respect. The International Student Office could be an outlier.

Yet international offices play a crucial role: they provide international students with the critical I-20 form and are the link between international students and the USCIS (United States Citizenship and Immigration Services). The I-20 is the legal document that you need to bring (the original signed copy) for your visa interview. When you receive your I-20 form, make sure to check the document letter by letter and digit by digit, because mistakes are common. I have experienced this firsthand. I received my I-20 and did not encounter any difficulties entering the United States. However, a few months later, the DMV office could not issue me a state ID because they noticed my birth year was listed incorrectly on the I-20 as 1998—far too young even for an undergraduate, let alone a master's student. So, deal with the university's international office very patiently and take the initiative to ensure your documents are accurate.

Do Your Research

I always recommend that international students do careful research before choosing a university. I once met an international graduate student who used Google

Maps to find a graduate school within driving distance of his relatives in Chicago. He applied to one that was three hours away and was accepted. Only after he arrived on campus did he realize that the school was located in the middle of nowhere and that it would be difficult to make a weekend trip to Chicago.

There are many things to consider as you search for a graduate school. Think about the safety of the campus and the location of the city. Try to find a grad program where students of similar backgrounds have already been admitted. If a graduate student from a particular country has been accepted to a program and performed well, faculty at that institute may notice how knowledgeable and hard-working they are and the selection committee may prefer to accept more applicants from that particular country and undergraduate institute.

Visa Application

The most common international student visa category is the F-1 student visa. However, if you are sponsored by an external funding source, you will be admitted on a J-1 visa. Applying for a student visa is a broad topic subject to rapid changes which I will just touch on briefly. Consult with your home country American embassy or the consular office for your visa requirements.

It is not advisable for F-1 students to apply for a student visa before receiving the I-20 document. Once you have received your legal documents, start applying for visa interviews. Make sure you pay your SEVIS fee (Student and Exchange Visitor Information System). American embassies and consular offices in different countries have different wait times for visa approval process. Unfortunately, some countries have a wait time of more than a year. If a long visa interview backlog appears to be affecting your university admission, try to request an early date from your home country consular office. If you are unable to secure an early date, contact your graduate program coordinator and ask about the possibility of deferring your admission to the next term or academic year. American visa interviews are unique as a visa officer usually takes less than 5 minutes to interview the student and will accept or reject the application in front of them. Bring all of your required documents — including your I-20, letter of acceptance, proof of funds, academic qualification and all information and documentation required by the visa office — to the interview.

Perhaps you might think that applying to a foreign university, receiving an I-20, and applying for a visa seems like too complex a task. You are not wrong. However, it is a challenge that you should undertake to make your life successful tomorrow. And you are not alone. Thousands of international students are admitted to American graduate schools every year. There are many hurdles along your way. This book is written to provide guidance to applicants who need information. Believe in yourself. You can do it!

References

- Foreign-born STEM employees and students in US (https://www.nsf.gov/nsb/sei/one-pagers/Foreign-Born.pdf).

- World Education Services (www.wes.org).

- US Fulbright scholarship (https://us.fulbrightonline.org/)

CHAPTER 15

GRAD APPLICATION TIMELINE

Graduate school admission is a long process. The doctoral application process might take close to a year. There are a lot of components to complete, and you need to plan accordingly. The application plan in this chapter is a generic one and may not be applicable to everyone. For example, if you completed your GRE and any other standardized tests last year and are satisfied with your score(s), you can start the application process a little later. If you have not started applying yet, this would be a good model to guide you in planning your graduate application timeline.

Most doctoral programs schedule their main enrollment in fall (autumn). For-profit universities and some public and nonprofit private schools have doctoral enrollment in spring, but this is not very common. Master's degree programs usually enroll two or three batches of students per calendar year (fall, spring, and summer). This model timeline is designed for a candidate whose target is fall enrollment. If you plan to start a graduate program (especially doctoral program) next year fall, it is safe to start your preparation this year summer. Let's see how we can arrange the steps.

On your mark - Summer

Summer is the best time to start applying for grad school admission the following fall (especially for doctoral programs). You can start by shortlisting doctoral schools and deciding how many doctoral schools you want to apply to. I would say choosing five to ten doctoral schools is safe. The more you apply to, the better. You do not lose anything (except the cost of the application fees) by applying to more schools, and it is far better to receive multiple admission offers than none.

If you are thinking of contacting a graduate school, summer is the best time. Faculty are usually on nine or ten-month contracts, which means they are not paid by the university during summer unless they conduct summer research. Hence, they might not be readily available to you to contact during summer. However, the graduate coordinator position is usually a year-round paid position. This person is typically a faculty member and serves on the selection committee. Graduate program coordinators are usually available online during the summer because they have to communicate with incoming graduate students. Even if you reach out a year in advance, the graduate coordinator should be available to give you more details. So, contact them, ask for more information, share your information, and perhaps the program coordinator would be kind enough to connect you with the faculty who conduct research that you are interested in.

I applied to my master's in the US from my home country Sri Lanka. My graduate program coordinator and I exchanged emails 24 times. Even though there was a ten-hour time difference between her and me, she always replied to me within 24 hours. She rushed to admit me to the program, but when I came to the US she was not in the department. Later I learned she rushed to admit us because she had to leave the department for medical treatments. I miss her dearly. The same thing happened for my doctoral application. I was admitted late to the program, and the graduate coordinator did not have funding available. But she quickly negotiated with the department to arrange funding for me, and I had uninterrupted funding for four years. I miss my doctoral coordinator and my supervisor dearly too. Try to maintain professional and honest relationships with graduate program coordinators; if they like you, they will support you above and beyond.

Test Preparation

Additionally, during summer you should prepare for and take your standardized test(s). This may take a month or two—it all depends on your target score and effort. Begin by reading all the instructions provided by the testing organization (e.g., ETS for the GRE) and plan your exam accordingly. If you have a few undergraduate colleagues who are also preparing for grad school, you can study for the tests together.

Again, let me remind you: there is no cut off mark or score for the GRE, GMAT, or LSAT. If you have a low undergraduate GPA, this could be a substitute that satisfies your selection committee to a certain extent. If you completed your undergraduate degree a long time ago, having a high standardized test score could convince your selection committee that your learning ability is good and you are well prepared for graduate studies.

If you are an international candidate applying from a non-English speaking country, you have to take language competency exams. There are many of them, but the most widely accepted tests are the TOEFL and the IELTS (see additional information on language proficiency tests in the international students chapter). Language proficiency does have a cutoff, unlike standardized tests, like the GRE. Different graduate programs maintain different cutoff marks. You can find your required language proficiency band or range on your graduate program website.

Get set - Fall

It is advisable to inform your recommender or ask their willingness to write you a recommendation ahead of time. Usually, faculty are back to work from August 1st, so you can e-mail your preferred faculty after August 1st. Try to avoid communicating with faculty during the first week of university, a very busy time, and ask them for a recommendation either before or after the first week. Refer back to the recommendation letters chapter for more information.

If you are applying to a master's program or a doctoral program without funding, late summer or early fall is a good time to start looking for external funding. Different funding sources have different deadlines.

SOP

Writing your statement of purpose (SOP) might take a considerable amount of time, so start early. Identify your top choice grad school and draft your SOP accordingly. Once you draft your SOP, let it rest until your emotional connection to the letter fades (this might take a week or two). After your emotional bond is gone, it will be easy to change and edit your SOP, since you can read and understand it as an outsider. After all the changes and modification, send it to someone who can give you constructive criticism. I would recommend asking your undergraduate or master's supervisor for their feedback. After his or her feedback and updates, send your SOP to an editor. Do not spent more than a month completing your SOP.

Diversity Statement and Teaching Philosophy

Fall is also the time to prepare your diversity statement and research statement. In the education field, graduate programs might also ask you to submit a teaching philosophy or teaching statement. If you are applying to multiple graduate programs and any of them request those statements, draft them. Read the statements carefully again and again, edit, share them with one or two of your supportive faculty, and send them to an editor for final edits. Try not to spend more than two weeks on these documents.

If you need to improve your standardized test scores or language test scores, you can re-take the exam(s) at this time. Many doctoral programs' applications are due December 1st. Start applying to your selected grad programs no later than two weeks prior to the deadline. For rolling enrollment, apply as soon as possible. After the application has been initiated, start sending the transcripts, original test results, and recommendation request. If you are eligible for an application fee waiver, apply for those without delay. If you are a potential candidate, you will most likely receive an invitation for a virtual interview at the end of the fall or the beginning of spring.

Spring – Go

From the beginning of spring, you will start receiving acceptance letters, waitlist notices, and rejection letters. This is also the time you will receive invitations for university visits. If you have received multiple offers, you can wait until you complete your campus visit to accept or turn down your offer. If you are fully sure about what to accept, do not wait until the last moment. There might be a wait list for the same offer. If you turn down your offer, an applicant who has the same ambition of attending their dream grad school might get admitted to the program.

If you are on a wait list, you can search the grad student portal. The grad cafe (www.thegradcafe.com) is a portal where grad students share their grad school application status for popular grad schools and graduate programs. Keep your eyes on such portals and do not wait too long to accept an offer. If you do not respond by the deadline, the university may decide to offer your opportunity to someone else.

Communicate

After accepting an offer you have to start communicating with the grad school and the program personnel. Usually, the graduate school and the graduate program you applied to are two disjoint entities and their communication (between the two entities) may not be strong. Whatever you want to communicate you should communicate to both parties.

You will receive a contract letter if you are offered a teaching assistant (TA) or research assistant (RA) position. Read the contract very carefully for information, such as number of credits available (30 is great), stipend (amount you are paid), mandatory school fees (these are non-tuition fees that you have to pay), required minimum GPA (if your GPA drops below the threshold you will lose your TA), and job duties (how many classes you will TA). If everything looks OK to you, you can accept and sign your contract. If you have any doubts, contact your graduate coordinator or the department's contact person. Do not forget to reach out to future colleagues you met during your grad school visit. Use their help and support to find housing.

Housing

Some apartment complexes in college towns ask their tenants to renew their leases as early as April. Hence, if you accept an offer by February, you have a substantial amount of time to find a good place to live. Ask for help and input from current students. They know in general what housing is best for grad students. I remember when I was pursuing my master's, I could see an apartment complex right across the road from my lab. Starting Wednesday nights, students would party there with music and dancing. This fun time would go on until Sunday afternoon. That might have been an awesome place for undergraduates to live, but such a place might be too much for a graduate student.

Relocation

Many recently accepted grad school students ask whether their relocation is paid by the university. In general, graduate schools do not fund relocation expenses. However, there is no harm in asking. Some specific fellowships allocate some money for doctoral student relocation. Some graduate schools have relocation funds available for incoming grad students with financial hardship. Read the grad office information. Such funding may be available from the grad school, the office of the Provost, or the graduate program. Read their websites for such information and apply immediately if you have a financial hardship.

Final thoughts

Thank you very much for reading this book. I salute you for your great passion and courage to in applying to graduate school. More than half of all bachelor's degree holders think one day they will pursue a PhD, but only a few actively pursue doctoral studies. Many recently graduated undergrads think one day they will pursue their MBA or anther master's degree, but only a few apply to grad school.

My journey as a master's and a doctoral student had many ups and downs. But when I look back, it was a remarkably rewarding six years of my life. I have never regretted the time and effort my graduate studies involved. During graduate school, I met awesome people, participated in research and academic publications, and even was published in many peer-reviewed journals and book chapters. I made my footprint in academic world. Not many have done that. Only around 14 percent of US population attains a graduate or professional degree, and less than 2 percent of the US population holds a doctoral degree (according to the US world population review). Earning a graduate degree feels like reaching the top of the world.

By reading this book from the beginning to the end, you have demonstrated your motivation to pursue a quality graduate education. I wish you great success in your future and the best of luck in attending your dream grad school!

Reference

- The grad cafe (www.thegradcafe.com).

- US world population review (https://worldpopulationreview.com/)

CHAPTER 16

CONCLUSION

Pursuing a graduate-level degree (master's or doctoral) is not only about advancing your academic credentials. It is also about elevating your career, your professional image, your professional and social credentials, and your overall standard of life. Higher education can provide you with opportunities to deepen your expertise and expand the boundaries of your knowledge and wisdom. While the journey of applying to grad school can be challenging, nothing rewarding is easy.

Imagine the day you received your undergraduate acceptance letter. Remember how excited you were to be admitted to a college. You might have had an awesome experience in your college. Think about the education you received there. Think about the peers, colleagues, teachers, and experts you met and the other people you connected with there. I understand and agree that earning an undergraduate degree is hard. But you made it! And look at your situation today. Think about the opportunities and benefits you have received because of your undergraduate degree. Compare your situation with the situation of a person who only complete his or her high school diploma. Examine the differences between your life and theirs, and consider that those differences have been influenced by your undergraduate degree.

Some people (mostly those who do not have an undergraduate degree) complain that an undergraduate degree is not worth the cost. However, it has been proven that individuals with an undergraduate degree earn significantly higher annual salaries than individuals who do not have an undergraduate qualification. Likely you heard such demotivating sentiments when you were younger, but nothing stopped you from pursuing an undergraduate degree. Today you are enjoying the harvest of what you sowed. The same applies to the graduate school. People may discourage you from pursuing a graduate degree. My advice for you is this: use the same argument that motivated you to pursue your undergraduate qualification. Despite the negativity, you pursued your degree and are happy with it. The same is applicable to your graduate qualification as well. Leave behind the negative noise and start pursuing your graduate qualification today. You will enjoy the lucrative benefits in the future.

Times have changed. A few decades ago, an average American man who only earned a high school diploma could have a decent job, buy a good vehicle, marry a woman, raise a family, and build a house—all on just one salary. That sounds like a sweet dream in today's world. We are at a turning point in American society where middle range salaried jobs require a bachelor degree, but, for promotions, employers seek graduate level qualifications. A terminal degree is now required to reach the top of the career level in many fields. Of course there are some exceptions, but remember that if someone has better academic qualifications, they can advance one step further than people who do not have such qualifications.

You need to believe in yourself. Everyone has hesitations about pursuing a graduate degree. The most common concern is not knowing an ideal time to go to grad school. The right thing to do is to start applying to grad school without delay. Initiate today, and never give up. Trust that university systems are designed to help you achieve your goals.

The majority of higher education institutions can provide you with a top-quality graduate education. While this book was written to help students get accepted to US graduate schools (for both competitive master's and doctoral studies), these instructions also apply to the admission process of graduate schools globally. Enjoy your remarkable graduate education journey which opens the doors to a sea of opportunities.

We highly value your feedback on this book. To help enhance the quality of this material, or if you find any information that needs to be reviewed or edited, please reach out at tulli@learnwithtulli.com, and for more updates please visit learnwithtulli.com.

REVIEW

If you found this book helpful, please scan the QR code below to share your thoughts. Your review can help others start their own journey towards academic success.

scan the QR code below to go to the Amazon page and leave your review.

ACKNOWLEDGMENTS

I convey my heartfelt gratitude to my wonderful readers and reviewers. Your thoughtful comments, emails, and reviews motivate me and empower me in my writing endeavors. Your trust in this book and your commitment to achieving your academic aspirations are truly inspiring. Throughout the process of writing this book, many individuals motivated and educated me on how to write a book effectively. I deeply appreciate their support.

I extend my heartfelt thanks to my mentors, advisors, students, and colleagues who have provided invaluable experience, guidance, feedback, and encouragement throughout my academic journey. I am particularly thankful for all the students, faculty, and staff of Eastern Illinois University, Indiana University – Bloomington,

238

Ivy Tech Community College in Columbus, IN, and the University of Cincinnati. The exposure I gained from these institutions immensely helped me in writing this book, as they provided me with a great academic and professional environment.

I convey my sincere gratitude to all the staff of the System Development & Improvement Center of University of Cincinnati for maintaining an awesome work environment.

Colleen Pawlicki and Troy Street Professional Services did a tremendous job editing this book. Varuna Prasad formatted this book very nicely, and Alishba Shah designed the great cover. Thank you very much for your support. I could not have made this book a high-quality product without your help.

I would like to thank my mom, dad, and sister for believing in me and motivating me throughout my long academic career. Thank you for your love and support. Last but not least, I am greatly thankful to my husband, Trent, for being a great source of strength and emotional support. Thank you very much.

Made in the USA
Las Vegas, NV
21 September 2024

95609635R00152